JANE'S RAILWAY YEAR

EDITED BY MURRAY BROWN

JANE'S

Above: Steam in the incomparable West Highlands. SRPS NBR 0-6-0 No 673 *Maude* runs past Lochailort with a returning excursion from Arisaig to Fort William on 28 May. No 673 had set out for Mallaig but was stopped short at Arisaig due to loss of time and a spate of lineside fires. *(Les Nixon)*

Title Page: National news in 1984 was dominated by the pit strike. Some coal did move, though, especially from the Nottinghamshire coalfield, where miners worked almost normally. This is 58001 taking an mgr service up the Erewash Valley line on 9 May. *(Gavin Morrison)*

First published in the United Kingdom in 1985 by Jane's Publishing Company Limited 238 City Road, London EC1V 2PU

ISBN 0 7106 0338 X

Designed by Bernard Crossland

Printed in the United Kingdom by Netherwood Dalton & Co Ltd Huddersfield

CONTENTS

BR MOTIVE POWER	**4**
BR MULTIPLE UNITS	**36**
BR COACHING STOCK	**59**
BR AND PO WAGONS	**66**
BR NETWORK	**70**
BR TRAFFIC	**95**
LRT AND METROS	**127**
PRESERVATION	**131**
STEAM ON BR	**159**
A RAILWAY DIARY FOR 1984	**171**

INTRODUCTION

While 1984 produced its usual quota of change and development on Britain's railways, the year was dominated by one particular issue, the miners' strike.

This bitter dispute was much more than an industrial issue and it was probably too much to expect that the traditionally close fraternal ties between organised labour in the rail and coal industries could be cast aside. As a result of the rail unions' support for the NUM strike action, BR's finances were hit hard, customer confidence was eroded, particularly in the Railfreight sector, and the industry dealt itself a severe blow at a time when national faith in rail transport was in the ascendant.

On a more positive note 1984 witnessed the long-awaited Government approval for electrification of the East Coast Main Line. The go-ahead was also given to wire up the important North London LMR-ER link to allow through electric working of freight traffic to and from the growing GE 25kV ac network.

The year will also be remembered as one when the railway showed first signs of being more colourful as BR's business sectors and the PTEs sought to catch the public eye. Spearheading this trend was the APT-style InterCity Executive colour scheme adopted for the successfully launched 'Gatwick Express' service, featured on our front cover. Similar colours were introduced to West Coast Main Line InterCity equipment, while ScotRail devised its own adaptation of this livery for its Glasgow-Edinburgh 47/7s and stock. The PTEs responsible for suburban services in Glasgow, Manchester and West Yorkshire in 1984 also introduced or applied more widely their own colour schemes for vehicles deployed on supported services.

Major changes on the signalling front were also recorded during the year as the traditional semaphore yielded to power signalling in centres like Chester and Westbury. By way of contrast, in Scotland the Kyle Line was turned over to the radio signalling which may prove the saviour of many lightly-used provincial routes.

July saw an end to the traditional direct involvement in shipping services by Britain's railways when Sealink was sold to Sea Container Services for £66m as part of the Government's privatisation policy.

The Severn Valley Railway's 1984 opening of its Kidderminster extension was an outstanding achievement for a private railway. Elsewhere, an apparently insatiable appetite for locomotives to restore directed the attention of preservationists to the long-neglected area of British locomotives built for overseas service, and giants from Greece and South Africa made their way home for an honourable retirement. A new feature towards the rear of this edition of *Jane's Railway Year* is a railway diary for 1984 compiled by Howard Johnston. The editor hopes that this, together with what follows, provides a lasting and entertaining record of a lively railway year.

MURRAY BROWN

Peterborough
April 1985

ACKNOWLEDGEMENTS

It is the Editor's and Publisher's pleasure to thank everyone who submitted material for this eventful year, including those whose work did not find a place in the book. Grateful acknowledgement is also due to the many individuals both within BR and outside who have co-operated in providing much information to make this book possible.

Photographic contributions
We will be delighted to consider 1985 material for the fifth edition, and good quality black and white prints not previously offered to other railway publications should be forwarded well packed to the Editor. There is a very limited amount of colour required – please contact the Editor before submitting transparencies. The full address for contributions is:
  The Editor
  Jane's Railway Year
  Jane's Publishing Company Ltd
  238 City Road
  London EC1V 2PU

BR MOTIVE POWER AND ROLLING STOCK

Inevitably the diminishing ranks of Class 40s attracted much enthusiast attention during 1984, but the type just hung on to see in another year, as the following review shows.

After more than two decades of service the Class 46s retired from the BR scene with the exception of two locomotives retained for Departmental use. This was the first main line class to pass into history with negligible interest from enthusiasts or the preservation movement.

Perhaps the less said the better on Class 58, deliveries of which continued during the year. Its teething troubles were the subject of comment when Railfreight Director Henry Sanderson named No 58020 after its birthplace. Meanwhile construction of the newest locomotive type for BR, the Class 89, was well under way at Crewe by the year-end, even though no-one seemed really sure if they still wanted it.

After several years of bad publicity the APT redeemed itself when it blazed out of 1984 with a record-shattering run from Euston to Edinburgh. On the multiple-unit front the unveiling of the BRE-built Class 150 prototypes and the entry into service of the Class 141 railbus heralded a massive transformation in the dmu fleet, while two pillars of railway society made their final runs. The good-looking Class 124 'Trans-Pennine' units and their Class 123 sisters said farewell, and the 30-year old Class 506 units passed away on 7 December amid a detonator salute.

Refurbishment and life-extension of emus continued during 1984 with examples of Class 303 emerging resplendent and the first Class 309 'Clacton' set entering Wolverton to be treated. Besides emus, Mk 3 coaches were also undergoing refurbishment – don't the years pass quickly – but the biggest surprise of all was the unveiling of 12 Mk 1 vehicles in Executive livery and with upgraded interiors mainly for charter and excursion work. The transformation achieved led commentators to question why such work had not been undertaken years earlier.

Enjoy it while you can! 'Whistler' fans appear to be the principal clients on the 1340 Blackpool-Newcastle service as it passes Poulton No 3 box behind No 40194 on 18 August. *(Les Nixon)*

'Whistler' rundown

It was a bad year for Class 40 afficionados for by 31 December 1984, only 17 remained in service with 33 being condemned in the period under review. The star working of the year was the 0830 Manchester Piccadilly-Skegness and the 1324 return. Famous celebrity locomotives were withdrawn including No 40001 and the Great Train Robbery machine, 40126. The flagship of the class, D200, was in much demand for railtours, confirming BR's wise decision to reinstate it to service in 1983, although it diced with death during the year when it was in a collision. Despite their dwindling numbers, Class 40s continued to roam and Severn Tunnel Junction and March still welcomed the class throughout the year, as did Scotland. Sadly, the end was in sight but it was to be a prolonged end, for BR confirmed that D200 would continue to run after its sisters were condemned. It seems certain that only three or four Class 40s are likely to survive as BR was putting a high price on recoverable components, pushing the purchase price far in excess of what could comfortably be raised by preservationists. Thus as 1984 drew to a close, it seemed certain that Nos 40106, preserved at Loughborough, 40145, preserved at Bury, D200 and possibly 40046 at Moreton-on-Lugg, the latter being used by the Ministry of Defence, would be the only survivors of this outstanding class in the years to come.

Above: Throughout the year the Sunday 4M19 1330 Heaton Carriage Sidings-Manchester Red Bank non-passenger-carrying coaching stock (NPCCS) train regularly provided a 'Whistler'. Pounding up Ferryhill bank on 7 October is the famous No 40009 which incredibly defied the laws of condemnation until 5 November when it met its end due to rough riding reports. This last vacuum-braked 40 frequently worked to the North East and it will be missed. It will also be missed by the Dart Valley Railway, whose General Manager had been patiently waiting for it to be withdrawn prior to tendering for this machine. Its failure with a serious fault, together with the fact that it was fitted with a Mk IV engine block which was required for further use, precluded preservation for this veteran. *(Peter J Robinson)*

Left: In 1984 No 40122/D200 went everywhere except where it should have been – on the Settle & Carlisle. The green 40 was used extensively on specials and on freight workings during 1984 and it was following a freight turn that D200 was in collision with Class 47 No 47107 at Guide Bridge in the early hours on 17 September. The 47 came off worse but D200 suffered a full length bodyside dent and lost a sandbox. It returned to Carlisle for remedial attention and, later in the year, was given a repaint at Upperby depot. This is the somewhat dented D200 standing on Longsight depot on 18 September waiting movement to Carlisle. *(Chris Thorp)*

Above: No 40122/D200 heads through Hexthorpe Sidings, Doncaster on 31 May with the 4M22 0930 Cleethorpes - Manchester Longsight NPCCS train, the return working of the 0215 newspaper train from Manchester. This was one of the rare occasions that this locomotive covered this particular working, which up to October was a regular Class 40 duty. The months since saw Class 47s and 31s handling most of the workings. *(David Ware)*

Centre: After many months of arranging and well deserving its place in *JRY* is this historical line-up of the first three Class 40s at Carlisle Kingmoor depot. At the time of this picture taken on 18 August, both Nos 40001 and 40002 were condemned but, even so, it was not an easy job to accomplish this memorable scene. *(Neville E Stead)*

Right: What a waste. The longest surviving Class 40 with continuous service, No 40001 was condemned at Carlisle on 23 July. Its defect? A worn pony wheel! This locomotive might well have stood a chance of preservation in view of its service record and its distinction of having worked the first-ever diesel-hauled 'Flying Scotsman' on 21 June 1958. Latter years saw it relegated to mundane duties such as this engineer's train from Crofton depot approaching Wakefield Kirkgate on 11 February. *(Colin Keay)*

Left: No 40181 had the distinction of working the last run of the 1324 Skegness-Manchester in 1984 and the last ever run on it by a Class 40 on 15 September. It is seen approaching Wainfleet with appropriate headboard and hundreds of contented passengers. A survey of passengers on this train revealed 367 enthusiasts and 109 'ordinary' passengers. *(B J Beer)*

Centre: With one of the top headboards for 1984, No 40086 pauses at Sheffield with the 0830 Manchester-Skegness train on 8 September. The headboard was provided by some genuine railway buffs from Stockport and was trial-fitted on No 40035 at Longsight prior to being carried on No 40086. *(Ian S Mitchell)*

Below: Another celebrity machine which came to the end of its life in 1984 was No 40028, the erstwhile *Samaria*. It was withdrawn in November with power unit troubles. A month earlier No 40028 was employed on the 'Cumbrian Whistler' railtour which worked down the Cumbrian coast line as far as Maryport. The tour took place on 6 October and the special is seen meandering along the coast at Parton. *(Peter J Robinson)*

50s in the news

Left: This is No 50041 *Bulwark* looking slightly better than it did in November 1983 when on the 23rd of that month it careered into Paddington station on its side. Throughout 1984 this machine was extensively rebuilt and it underwent a classified repair at the same time. By the year-end it was finished and painted, ready for a trial run. This picture was taken in October, when most of the bodywork repairs had been completed. *(Gavin Morrison)*

Centre: An abundance of heavy freight power due to the miners' strike did not prevent the unusual employment of No 50003 *Temeraire* on the 1521 Nottingham-Birmingham Lawley Street Freightliner on 17 August. The interloper is seen passing Clay Mills, near Burton-on-Trent. *(John Tuffs)*

Below: BR's 'Conway Crusader' railtour of 10 March brought No 50018 *Resolution* to new territory when it traversed the scenic Conway Valley line to Blaneau Ffestiniog. A rerun of the tour on Easter Saturday, 21 April gave customers and photographers an even more memorable feast with the unrepeatable combination of green 'Hoover' No 50007 *Sir Edward Elgar* and Class 40 No 40192. The pair were photographed on the branch at Roman Bridge. *(John Whitehouse)*

Above: What's green and does 'the ton'? No 50007, formerly *Hercules* and now *Sir Edward Elgar*, following a February repaint and renaming that brought very mixed reactions from Class 50 followers. On 27 April *Edward* was on NE/SW duties and is seen drawing away from Gloucester with the 1355 Cardiff Central-Leeds. *(Peter J C Skelton)*

Below: While No 50007 hogged most of the Class 50 limelight in 1984, those remaining members of the class to sport the 'original' livery went to Doncaster for overhaul and a repaint in large logo livery. The three that saw in 1984 were Nos 50001, 50013 and 50047. No 50013 *Agincourt* was the last to be treated, going north in May and returning to traffic on 11 September. This is 50047 *Swiftsure*, first of the trio to fall, coming off the Salisbury line at Redbridge on 5 February with the diverted Sunday 0945 Exeter St Davids-Waterloo. *(John Chalcraft)*

BR's move from corporate to sector identity began to take a tangible form on the West Coast Main Line in May when Class 87 No 87012 *Coeur-de-Lion* emerged from Willesden depot in a derivation of the Executive livery adopted for two WR HSTs and the Gatwick Express stock. Although a WCML Mk 3 stock refurbishment programme had already been announced, there were few matching vehicles available for the inaugural down 110 mph 'Royal Scot', seen being led out of Euston by *Coeur-de-Lion* on 14 May. *(Mick Roberts)*

New look WCML electrics

Willesden depot staff also painted No 87006 *City of Glasgow* in this smart style with a predominance of graphite grey to allow comparison with 87012, but it received an early 'thumbs down'. This locomotive too participated in the launch of 110 mph WCML services and was captured on film north of Norton Bridge with the up 'Royal Scot' on 14 May. *(Hugh Ballantyne)*

Above: The first Class 86 to receive Executive livery was No 86242 *James Kennedy GC*, which was finished with the darker grey band extended onto the nose and the cab window surrounds. It is seen approaching South Kenton on 9 August with the 1515 Manchester Piccadilly-Euston. *Below:* This variation was soon followed by the painting in similar style of Class 87 No 87009 *City of Birmingham*. As the nameplates straddled the three bands of colour, BR's Director of Industrial Design, Mr J Cousins, authorised their refitting in a position higher up the bodyside. This is No 87009, freshly repainted at Willesden on 3 September. *(Mick Roberts; Murray Brown)*

National pride

Above: The Scottish Region's bid for an independent identity reached new heights in October when push-pull-fitted Class 47/7 No 47708 *Waverley* emerged from BREL Crewe in ScotRail's own adaptation of the InterCity Executive livery. Before the year end an Edinburgh-Glasgow push-pull set had been finished in matching style and the rest of the dedicated fleet was to follow, including the four further 47s then earmarked for push-pull conversion. The photographer caught a resplendent *Waverley* at Gateshead on 1 November. *(Peter J Robinon)*

Below: For its naming *University of Stirling* at that city on 17 September No 47617 became only the fifth Class 47 to receive Class 50-style large logo and numerals. The handiwork was that of Eastfield depot staff, who must have had a few tins of paint left over, for in November Class 08 No 08938 was turned out with a very special finish which included yellow cab, light grey roof, dark grey body and red coupling rods and running board edging. This is No 47617 at Stirling on the occasion of its naming, which followed the opening of a new travel centre. *(Tom Noble)*

47 update

Above: Twenty-four Class 47s were converted to electric train-heating operation during 1984 with No 47627 emerging at the year end and No 47628 complete but not tested. Here is No 47625 *City of Truro*, formerly 47076, sparkling in ex-works condition at the head of 1Z24 0840 Blackpool-Halifax track recording special on 28 November. The location is Mytholmroyd. *(F J Bullock)*

Below: Way back in 1967, Class 47s, or Brush Type 4s by which they were known, worked some of the Waterloo-Bournemouth services. Nos D1923-27 officiated but, since then, no locomotives of this type have been rostered into Waterloo . . . . until 1984. On 14 May and the start of the summer timetable a Class 47 was booked for the 1900 Portsmouth and Southsea-Waterloo van train. In addition, the 0140 Waterloo-Exeter and the 0645 return were rostered for the same power. The latter train is pictured near Dinton behind Class 47/4 No 47525 on 6 September. *(G F Gillham)*

End of the 46s

The unloved Class 46 came to the end of its reign on BR in November. However, considering that the class has survived for over two decades, it would be wrong to place it in the category of unsuccessful. The 46s received extensive refurbishment at Brush in the late 1960s and latter years saw the remaining survivors concentrated at Gateshead depot. The final year witnessed business as usual for the eleven which saw in the new year, but as 1984 progressed individual machines were condemned. There was little interest from the preservationists' point of view although one request was received from a prospective buyer. BR imposed a huge price for one of these machines as the bogies, wheelsets and power units were classed as recoverable items and were therefore subject to a value far in excess of pure scrap. The final survivors made their way to Doncaster Works for scrapping instead of the graveyard at Swindon. This portfolio reflects the final year in BR revenue service for the Class 46, although it is not quite the end for two locomotives: Nos 46035 and 46045 were despatched to Derby after withdrawal on 25 November for further use in Departmental guise under the Research & Development Division.

Right: The flagship of the class, No 46026 *Leicestershire and Derbyshire Yeomanry* (known by many fans as 'LADY'), worked its final train on 17 November when it substituted a Class 40 on the 'Grampian Highlander' railtour organised by RESL. The Class 46 worked the train into Newcastle where two Class 31s took over for the run north. No 46026 had main generator problems and also two traction motors were giving cause for concern. It is true to say that Gateshead staff were sorry that this celebrity machine did not last the course to the very end but there comes a time when enough is enough. Indeed, Gateshead depot staff are to be credited with exemplary work in keeping these aged machines running for so long, bearing in mind that the survivors had not seen the inside of a BREL works for over five years. Here is No 46026 at 0435 hours at Newcastle on its final train. *(R Trinder)*

Below: Various rumours circulated during the year that the survivors were to be withdrawn en masse but it was not until 25 November that this finally occurred. There was only one farewell tour, organised by Pleasure Rail, and this took place on 17 June involving a tour of lines on the Southern Region and utilising No 46026. Here the 'Class 46 Tribute' leaves Wimbledon. *(Alex Dasi-Sutton)*

Right: Summer traffic to the West Country took the Class 46s to their old haunts and the long journey from the north did not prove too taxing. This is No 46011 rounding the tight curve leading to Gwinear Road level crossing heading the 0750 Bristol-Penzance on 12 September. On the right is the trackbed of the Helston branch. No 46011 succumbed at Margam in November and was taken straight to Swindon for breaking. (*John Whitehouse*)

Above: Besides the summer dated trains into Cornwall, the Speedlink service to St Blazey also brought Class 46s into the Duchy until their demise. On 29 February No 46027 leaves Tresulgar Viaduct while in charge of the 0915 St Blazey-Severn Tunnel Junction Air Braked Service (ABS), formed entirely of PBA china clay hoppers. (*John Chalcraft*)

Left: No 46027 passes Hinckley on 13 April hauling the newly introduced 7L53 Washwood Heath Sidings-ECC Croft Quarry stone empties. This locomotive had the distinction of being the last Class 46 in service, for it hauled stock from Newcastle to York on Monday 27 November (after official withdrawal date on the previous day) before continuing to Doncaster to be turned off for the last time. (*Paul A Biggs*)

Right: Class 58 spread its wings as more locomotives came off the production line and one of the more noteworthy exploits of this new class was the despatch for crew training purposes of brand new No 58014 to Reading. The main reason for this move was to train the men for the coal traffic from the Midlands to Didcot and the 58 made numerous test runs including hauling passenger vehicles to Oxford. In this picture No 58014 is seen in charge of a trial working approaching Oxford from the north on 19 September. Fifteen further Class 58s were ordered on 16 June at a total cost of £14.7m, bringing the total of the class delivered or on order up to 50. *(Rodney Lissenden)*

Below: A notable exercise was conducted with No 58014 during its WR stay when on 3 May the locomotive was utilised on a 'passenger turn'. In reality it was a run to Oxford and return from Old Oak Common with a rake of Mk 2ds for the benefit of motive power instructors. The Class 58 had run from Reading to pick up the stock and departed with the special at 1220. This photo shows the train at West Ealing. *(Colin J Marsden)*

58s gain groun

Below: The first recorded regular double-headed working for Class 58 locomotives occurred at the end of the year when for several days two locomotives were rostered for the Radcliffe-Fletton fly-ash trains. The reason for this was the lack of full maintenance cover at Toton depot and the attendant risk that should one locomotive fail, there would have been serious service disruptions. As it was, on one day one of the locomotives ran out of fuel, necessitating a special stop at the Peterborough fuelling point. This 28 December picture shows Nos 58009 and 58016 arriving at the Fletton fly-ash terminal with 6E54 from Radcliffe. *(John Rudd)*

Left: With little coal traffic on offer Toton's 58s followed their Class 56 cousins and found other work. This is No 58002 at Saltley, Birmingham powering the 1213 SO Lawley Street - Nottingham Freightliner on 7 July. *(Paul A Biggs)*

Left: In 1984 Class 58s got involved in dragging operations over the Birmingham-Nuneaton TV line due to Sunday engineering work on the Coventry - Birmingham line. On 10 June No 58013 was busy leading 86255 *Penrith Beacon* and the 0857 Wolverhampton-Euston past Abbey Junction, Nuneaton. *(Paul A Biggs)*

Below: Railtour participants also had access to Class 58 haulage in 1984. On 16 September No 58007 was in the limelight at Buxton with Hertfordshire Rail Tours' Midland Macedoine. *(Les Nixon)*

Early electrics go for scrap

Left: After languishing for many months at Crewe and Stoke, a convoy of blue asbestos-insulated ac electrics of Classes 82 and 83 were moved in a special working to Leicester for breaking by Vic Berry Ltd. Here the 14 locomotives are lined up by Humberstone Road Yard, Leicester on 27 September prior to being moved in threes into Berry's yard. The locomotives are Nos 83002, 83010, 83007, 83005, 83008, 82002, 82007, 83014, 83011, 83001, 83006, 83013, 82004 and 82006. *(R T Osborne)*

Left: A general view of Vic Berry's Leicester Yard, which began dismantling blue asbestos-lined vehicles in 1984. Pictured on 6 October are ac locomotives Nos 82002 (left), 83005 and 83008 awaiting breaking. In the background can be seen Class 03 shunter No 03079, which Berry's purchased to handle traffic within the yard. *(Paul A Biggs)*

Below: Although some ac electrics are now 25 years old, their modern looks lead one to imagine their scrapping is premature. It is interesting that some continental concerns have undertaken refurbishment schemes on earlier electric machines but BR has been reluctant to entertain this idea. No 83006 comes to the end of the road in Berry's yard on 5 October. *(Mike Spencer)*

GE 86s

Above: The new order came to the Great Eastern main line on Sunday evening 28 October when four Class 86 locomotives were hauled from Willesden to Stratford to begin crew training in preparation for the Anglia Electrification service commencing in May 1985. The four ac locomotives were Nos 86007, 86030, 86316 *Wigan Pier* and 86324. This picture shows the very first driver training run on 29 October with No 86316 operating from Thornton Fields to Colchester and return. The train is awaiting a path at Stratford while Class 315 unit No 315861 passes on the down local. *(Colin J Marsden)*

Below: Nos 86316 *Wigan Pier* and 86007 are seen at Shenfield on 20 November with the 0752 Thornton Fields-Colchester training run. Four runs in each direction were scheduled to operate from 29 October to 10 May. *(Ian Cowley)*

Above: Tinsley-based Class 45/0s Nos 45013 and 45022 *Lytham St Annes* were 'customised' during 1984 with the addition of white cab window surrounds, cantrail stripe and grille frames. This is how the treatment looked on No 45022, seen at Chinley East Junction on 1 September with Tunstead-Horton Road limestone hoppers. *(Steve Turner)*

45/0s in focus

Right: 10 September saw the surprise withdrawal of four Class 45/0 locomotives, Nos 45002, 45023, 45043 and 45050. No Class 45/0s had been withdrawn for some time but almost certainly as an indirect result of the miners' dispute there was no work for them and bogies were at a premium. Nos 45023/43/50 were at the time in Derby works and repairs ceased, while No 45002 was in working order at the time it was condemned. It is seen with less than one month's service left in charge of a Dee Marsh-Tinsley scrap train passing through Burton-on-Trent on 17 August. It will not come as a surprise if major inroads are made into the Class 45/0s in 1985. *(John Tuffs)*

Above: 'Stand up that boy who asked for two '99s' and a Raspberry Split!' One of the railway curiosities of 1984 involved Class 25/3 No 25322, which received the painted name *Tamworth Castle* and acquired a somewhat unorthodox livery which gained it an unofficial name – 'The Ice Cream Van'! The locomotive had been condemned but was renovated by apprentices at Tyseley depot and reinstated to capital stock. No 25322 is pictured at Tamworth High Level on 12 May with cinema coach ZDW 150353 during an exhibition staged in connection with Tamworth Rail Week, which marked the introduction on 14 May of the new two-hourly 'Midlands Link' between Birmingham and Nottingham. *(Steve Knight)*

Spruced-up Sulzers

Below: Mutton dressed as lamb? This colour study of Class 45/0 No 45022 *Lytham St Anne's* at Bristol Bath Road on 31 July shows the detail of Tinsley's paint job on the ageing lady. *(Geoff Cann)*

Far-flung 37s

Above: Laira's Cornish-based No 37207 *William Cookworthy* in March received embellishments to confirm its 'ownership' by Cornish Railways, the separate administration established to run the Duchy's network in July 1983 under the stewardship of Truro-based Mr 'Rusty' Eplett. This picture of 37207 at Par on 22 August with china clay hoods shows the legend 'Cornish Railways' and the crossed flags of BR and Cornwall on the nose, and the 'Cornish Lizard' device on the bodyside. *(Roger W Penny)*

Below: No 37264 shunts the stock of the 1220 to Fort William at Mallaig on 14 June. The West Highland saw service from the first reliveried examples both from Swindon and Crewe in 1984, 37264 being the first such machine to be turned out by Crewe. *(John Chalcraft)*

Left: During the year, 19 Class 25s were condemned, leaving only 94 to face an uncertain 1985. Certain that they would be condemned but uncertain of the date, enthusiasts provided some novel headboards on the Cambrian line in 1984, the winner being 'The Rat Catcher'. A simple commemorative headboard was provided for the final working of the class on the last day of the summer season, 15 September, when Nos 25034 and 25058 officiated with the 1400 Aberystwyth-Shrewsbury, pictured before departure and posing for a likely end of an era. *(D Jackman)*

Below: There was little in the way of Class 25 news in 1984. Apart from the bizarre painting, naming and re-instatement to service of No 25322 (see p21), the survivors of the Class soldiered on and it was to the Cambrian lines that 'Rat' fans made their way. There, despite the non-too-exhilarating performances of 1983, BR gave the class another chance in 1984 and on the whole they behaved well. It was generally believed that 1984 would be the final year of the Class 25s on the Cambrian summer trains, 1985 to see Class 37s take over. *JRY* will duly reveal all! On 21 July Nos 25279 and 25313 were put in charge of the 1010 Aberystwyth-Euston and the pair are seen at speed at Westbury, where the token is exchanged. *(John Whitehouse)*

Cambrian 'Rat' finale

20s break new ground

Class 20 spread its wings with a vengeance in 1984, with Toton-based examples penetrating the North West to handle Peak Forest and Wigan area traffic and the full potential of the class was belatedly realised, particularly with the fact that two locomotives in harness had more braking power than one Class 40/45 or 56. During the year there was a procession of Class 20s to BREL for dual-braking and because of the lengthy periods between classified repairs, locomotives were shopped specially for this modification. The summer exodus of pairs of 20s to the East Coast resort of Skegness continued as in previous years and the ScR yielded many of its long-allocation machines back to the LMR. This small review highlights the wandering 'Choppers'.

Top: The main (new) train working entrusted to Class 20s in 1984 was the Tunstead stone traffic, which was rostered for this class as from 14 May. Nos 20172 and 20077 power past Peak Forest with 6F43 1539 Tunstead-Oakleigh Sidings on 1 September. *(Paul D Shannon)*

Right: On 14 May, the first official day for Class 20 workings on the Tunstead to Northwich trains, Nos 20172 and 20170 are seen at Buxworth, near Chinley, heading the afternoon 6F43 train to Oakleigh Sidings, Northwich. *(John Tuffs)*

Right: Nuneaton saw its first Class 20s in May when examples arrived for crew training prior to use on the Abbey Street Sidings-Croft Quarry stone trains. Pictured at the north end of Nuneaton Trent Valley station on 16 May is No 20213. *(Paul A Biggs)*

Below: Highlight of the Class 20 railtour scene in 1984 was undoubtedly F&W's 'Devonshire Dart' which took a pair of 'Choppers' into the West Country for the first time. Meldon Quarry was the destination of this much-photographed train and here the valiant duo, Nos 20169 and 20184, prove they did it as they are seen at Meldon on 8 July. *(Steve Turner)*

Above: One of the highlights for enthusiasts of the 1984 timetable was the rostering of Class 20s on summer dated Scarborough trains. However, the joy was short-lived for the Tinsley-based 'Choppers' (not usually diagrammed for passenger service, unlike the Toton allocation which works the Skegness trains) rarely worked the diagram as booked. One day on which they did was 25 August, when Nos 20068 and 20054 were performing. The train is the 1520 Scarborough-Glasgow (which the 20s worked as far as York) and is seen passing Haxby Road Gates box. *(David Stacey)*

Below: The arrival at Wigan of Class 20s for crew training on 28 April set the scene for the first ever visit of a member of this class to Southport. No 20212 was given the unusual task of working 1L49 1700 Southport-Manchester and the train is seen waiting to depart on 28 August. By the time the train left Wigan, there were 35 people on board, of whom 26 were enthusiasts. *(R J Casselden)*

Above: At the beginning of the year there remained just six Class 56s to be completed by BREL Crewe and all entered traffic during 1984. This was the first of them, No 56130, which entered traffic on 31 March. On 9 May this 1984 product was occupied with a Lackenby-Corby steel working and is depicted nearing Trowell Junction, on the Erewash Valley line. During the nine months of 1984 in which the miners' strike was continuing, BR's heavy freight motive power fleet was severely underutilised, and the 56s were particularly hard hit. They consequently became a familiar sight on a wide range of work, including the Lackenby-Corby traffic, which they often worked in pairs in place of the previously regular brace of 37s. *(Gavin Morrison)*

56 deliveries

Above: During 1984 Class 56s became regular performers on the Lindsey-Preston Docks oil traffic. This is No 56010 just about to cross Strand Road, Preston on 29 June. *(Tony Woof)*

. . .completed

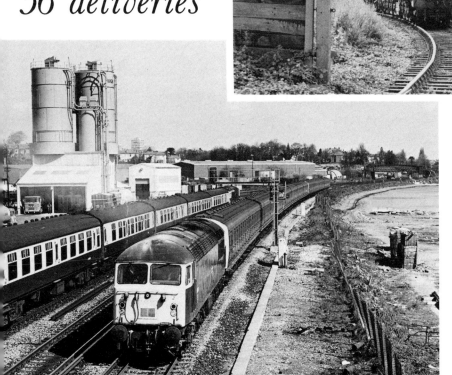

Left: In March the Southern Region embarked on a training programme for Eastleigh drivers on Class 56 locomotives. Initially No 56049 from Cardiff Canton was borrowed and a trailing load was formed of three condemned 4SUB units. The course lasted four days with one day in the classroom and three days practical training on a circuit embracing Eastleigh - Southampton - Salisbury - Basingstoke - Eastleigh. Passing Mount Pleasant Crossing between St Denys and Southampton is No 56034 on April 12 with 4SUB units Nos 4670, 4680 and 4742. *(Colin J Marsden)*

31/4s replace dmus

Above: Class 31/4 locomotives were entrusted with the new locomotive-hauled services between Manchester and Hull/Cleethorpes commencing on 14 May. At one stage, there was concern that insufficient locomotives would be converted by Doncaster Works in time but BREL came up with the goods. In addition, as dual-heated stock was required for the service, some Mk 2 vehicles were removed from the Norwich - Birmingham service and replaced by Mk 1s. On the first day of the new service, No 31406, one of the original Class 31/4 conversions, heads the 0941 Manchester-Hull through Ashburys. *(Kim Fullbrook)*

Left: With a mixture of Mk 1 and Mk 2 vehicles, the 1341 Manchester Piccadilly-Hull passes Chinley on 10 November with No 31404 at its head. *(Peter M Marsh)*

Above: The other service worked by the 'Trans-Pennine' units, that from Leeds to Morecambe, also reverted to Class 31/4 haulage. Three of these services started back at Hull with corresponding trains working through to Hull. Breasting Giggleswick bank is No 31405 powering the 0905 Hull-Lancaster on 6 October. The locomotive-hauled trains worked to Lancaster, with DMU services working through to Morecambe. *(Colin Keay)*

Below: The changeover to locomotive-hauled services on the Leeds-Lancaster route brought a welcome return to locomotives stopping at the once busy station of Hellifield. This Midland Railway edifice now under threat of demolition plays host to No 31410 on the 1550 Hull-Lancaster on 20 September. *(Gavin Morrison)*

Above: During 1984 13 Class 58 locomotives were completed at Doncaster with the year-end seeing No 58023 as the latest off the production line. However, some did return to Doncaster almost immediately (all good classes have their teething troubles!). This was the scene on 28 July when Nos 58016/17/18 and, nearest the camera, 58019 were under construction. *(Hugh Ballantyne)*

Workshop topics

Centre: The Class 31 electric train heat programme continued at Doncaster Works during 1984 with Nos 31433 to 31460 being completed. This general view was taken in March. In the background is Class 50 No 50019 undergoing Intermediate repair. *(Gavin Morrison)*

Right: A departure from the then standard eth conversion took place with No 31446 (ex-31316) when it was fitted with the headlamp modification. No 31446 was photographed on 1 June whilst undergoing Heavy General repair, dual braking and eth conversion, notwithstanding fire damage! However, one out of ten for effort for the headlamp placing. Considering how much work is spent on corporate image and livery details, a mockery is made of all this when a lamp can be just "stuck on the front". Was it really asking too much for it to be centrally placed? Only ten locomotives, Nos 31446-55, were fitted with the headlamp and, on reflection, thank goodness! *(David Ware)*

Right and below: Anything Glasgow can do, we can do better! So sang Swindon Works in 1984 when tradition and inconvenience were blown to the wind as several Class 27s made the long trek south for cannibalisation or repair. The two photographs depict one of 1984's more unusual sights with No 27017 (complete with Haymarket's Castle motif) awaiting attention outside the shops and No 27002 receiving medication inside. The first three, Nos 27002/19/36 arrived at Swindon on 27 April and were subsequently followed by Nos 27002/17/28/34/36/40. The photographs are dated 22 October. *(John Tuffs)*

"What is it, dad?". "Dunno, son, better ask your mother". This was all that visitors to Crewe Open Day on 2 June could see of the prototype Class 89 electric machine, the drag boxes of which were under construction. The completed locomotive is due to take to the rails in 1985. *(Gary Grafton)*

31

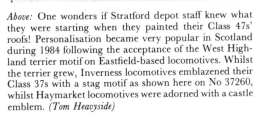

Above: One wonders if Stratford depot staff knew what they were starting when they painted their Class 47s' roofs! Personalisation became very popular in Scotland during 1984 following the acceptance of the West Highland terrier motif on Eastfield-based locomotives. Whilst the terrier grew, Inverness locomotives emblazened their Class 37s with a stag motif as shown here on No 37260, whilst Haymarket locomotives were adorned with a castle emblem. *(Tom Heavyside)*

Egged on by Gateshead's crests, Eastfield's terriers and Inverness's stag, Haymarket joined in the personalisation game by adding this castle motif to its Class 47s commencing in October 1984. No 47710 *Sir Walter Scott* was photographed on 15 November. *(Colin Boocock)*

Scottish style

Below: One of the most astonishing edicts to be made in 1984 came from BR's senior Scottish Region management who directed that the white stripes which adorned various Class 37s and one Class 27 belonging to Eastfield should be removed. Now there are tasteful embellishments and there are those that are not. Quite clearly, enthusiast opinion was very much in favour of the white stripe fleet and the enforcement order was even more surprising in that selected English machines had carried the white stripe officially for years (e.g. the Birmingham Class 104 DMUs which ran on the Blackpool line and some Finsbury Park Class 31/4s). In addition, the Eastern Region had its Anglo-Scottish BG vehicles specially painted with a white stripe in 1984! However, Eastfield's lot is not to reason why and the white stripes went. The last locomotive to carry them was No 37017, seen here proving the point that the stripe enhanced its appearance whilst heading the 1110 Kyle of Lochalsh-Inverness approaching Plockton on 25 April. This locomotive also gained further fame in 1984 when it assumed the title of Britain's most northerly-travelled locomotive. Gaining this honour entailed demolishing the buffer stops at Thurso on 16 June! *(Peter J Robinson)*

Right: Because of the failure of the Isle of Wight's Departmental shunter No 05001, alias 97804, a replacement was made in the form of condemned Gateshead Class 03 No 03079. It was moved to Eastleigh depot and resided there for several weeks prior to being shipped to the IoW on 8 April. By September the Class 03 was undergoing modification in Ryde depot where its cab and chimney were being cut down to enable it to work through Ryde tunnel, which has limited clearances. A rare view of a Class 03 at Eastleight is this picture showing No 03079 awaiting its new adventure on 26 February. *(John Chalcraft)*

Below: To shunt his Leicester yard Vic Berry purchased a Class 03 vacuum-braked shunter. This was No 03069, which had spent the last years of its BR life at Gateshead. It was moved to Leicester in a freight and is pictured being shunted on 4 January at Leicester, Humberstone Road yard by Class 08 No 08465. BR gave Vic's staff tuition in driving the 03 before it commenced duty shunting blue asbestos stock and the bogie recovery wagons which subsequently took the Commonwealth, B4 and B5 bogies to Stanway yard, Colchester for storage pending further use on refurbished vehicles. *(John Tuffs)*

03s on the move

Perhaps the most inevitable name to be bestowed in 1984 was *Gatwick Express* in view of the importance and publicity which BR gave to its most important new service of the year. Posing outside Stewarts Lane with depot staff and engineers from headquarters is No 73123. The staff had also produced the excellent headboard for the inaugural day. Also note the creative use of the headcode! The photo is dated 9 May, one day before the locomotive was officially named. *(Colin J Marsden)*

More names

For its naming *University of Stirling* on 17 September Class 47/4 No 47617 was duly repainted but with a difference. It received Class 50-style livery, joining push-pull sisters 47711 and 47712. Here Sir Kenneth Alexander (left), Principal of Stirling University, unveils the nameplate of No 47617 at Stirling on 17 September watched by Mr Chris Green, BR's Scottish General Manager. A new travel centre was opened prior to the ceremony. *(Tom Noble)*

1984 was the year when tradition and some would say respect and integrity went out of the window when it came to namings. BR in a number of instances went for names which they felt would appeal to the masses but of which the railway fraternity, wanting traditional railway names, were to disapprove. There was widespread criticism in the railway press over such names as *Top of the Pops*, and *Wigan Pier*, although some Wiganers were obviously pleased.

The full list of namings, totalling 41, was as follows:

43157 *Yorkshire Evening Post* 12 January
43049 *Neville Hill* 21 January
43095 *Heaton* 4 February
50007 *Sir Edward Elgar* 26 February
47408 *Finsbury Park* 10 March
43057 *Bounds Green* 10 March
43162 *Borough of Stevenage* 21 March
86328 *Aldaniti* 21 March
43047 *Rotherham Enterprise* 27 March
43100 *Craigentinny* 31 March
25322 *Tamworth Castle* April
43053 *County of Humberside* 10 April
86258 *Tallyllyn* 30 April
43110 *Darlington* 5 May
86245 *Dudley Castle* 8 May
73123 *Gatwick Express* 10 May
43061 *City of Lincoln* 12 May

43092 *Highland Chieftain* 15 May
43052 *City of Peterborough* 19 May
37229 *The Cardiff Rod Mill* 23 May
56133 *Crewe Locomotive Works* 2 June
47596 *Aldeburgh Festival* 8 June
43102 *City of Wakefield* 23 June
43105 *Hartlepool* 4 July
37078 *Teesside Steelmaster* 4 July
86315 *Rotary International* 4 July
37260 *Radio Highland* 6 July
43101 *Edinburgh International Festival* 23 August
43002 *Top of the Pops* 30 August
47611 *Thames* September
47618 *Fair Rosamund* September
86316 *Wigan Pier* 14 September
47617 *University of Stirling* 17 September
43077 *City of Nottingham* 20 September
43121 *West Yorkshire Metropolitan County* 23 September
86231 *Starlight Express* 1 October
43152 *St. Peter's School York AD 627* 5 November
47407 *Aycliffe* 8 November
08525 *Percy the Pilot* 8 November (wooden nameplates removed immediately afterwards)
58020 *Doncaster Works BREL* 12 November
47574 *Lloyds List* 11 December

Above: 1984's most controversial naming was that of Class 50 No 50007 which had its nameplates *Hercules* removed to be replaced by *Sir Edward Elgar*. It was also repainted into Brunswick Green with cast brass numberplates! Simon Rattle, Leader of the Birmingham Symphony Orchestra, performed the naming ceremony at Paddington on 25 February in remembrance of the 50th anniversary of the composer's death. The repainting and renaming caused considerable public comment, much of it hostile. Indeed, as the year drew to a close there were reports that BR was considering restoring the name *Hercules* to No 50007 and fitting the *Sir Edward Elgar* plates to a Class 47 locomotive – which is probably what should have been done in the first place! The pictures show the gleaming No 50007 passing Twyford in difficulty with the 1415 from Oxford-Paddington. The 50 worked the 1215 from Paddington to Oxford following the ceremony but suffered traction motor defects and on its return to London retired to Old Oak Common for medication. *(John Chalcraft)*

Above/right: 1984 saw another example of the curious BR habit of removing nameplates from existing named locomotives when Class 87 No 87023 lost it plates so the name *Highland Chieftain* could be given to HST power car No 43092 to mark the start of HST services to Inverness (see p109). Presumably the process gets reversed if the wires ever go north of Perth! These pictures show a bare-sided 87023 leaving Birmingham New Street on 11 August with the 1229 to Blackpool and one of the new plates fitted to power car No 43092. *(Tony Woof; Brian Cuttell)*

Highland Chieftain

BR MULTIPLE UNITS

'Sprinter' go-ahead

It was, to put it bluntly, a *fait accompli* year for the Class 150 dmu. The plan was to play off the two BREL-built prototypes against the two Metro-Cammell-built contenders for BR's dmu replacement programme. Serious difficulties which befell the building of the latter, particularly cab and bogie construction, so delayed the Metro-Cammell units that by the end of 1984 neither unit had emerged from the manufacturer's Saltley works. With an urgent wish to eradicate its blue asbestos-insulated dmu stock by the end of 1987, BR was soon seeking permission from the Transport Minister to authorise construction of further Class 150s, despite its unproven design. Fortunately, for once, BR appeared to have hit the jackpot with the prototype Class 150, for they practically had a job in getting unit No 150001 (fitted with the Cummins engine and Gmeinder final drive with Voith transmission) to fail.

Unit No 150002 with the Rolls Royce engine and Self Changing Gears gearbox did not perform in such an exemplary manner, however.

Even before the prototype was handed over on 8 June, tenders had been invited for 50 2-car versions and as the year ended, authorisation was awaited for a further 100 2-car units,

to be dubbed as 'Sprinters' by BR's Provincial Services sector to reflect the units' acceleration capabilities.

Thus the future pattern of the dmu fleet had been decided – Class 150 in either 2- or 3-car versions in the medium weight category and the twin railbus based on the Class 140 in the lightweight bracket.

Above: BREL Managing Director Philip Norman hands over the symbolic driver's key to prototype No 150001 to BRB Chairman Bob Reid at York Works on 8 June. *(Steve Chapman)*

Below: No 150001 passes Burton on Trent bound for the Railway Technical Centre at Derby on 29 August after trials between Lichfield and Bromsgrove earlier in the day. *(John Tuffs)*

Left: After extensive trials based on the Railway Technical Centre, Derby and undertaken predominantly on the Midland main line, the prototype Class 150 began public service on the Derby to Matlock branch on 5 November. This unit, fitted with the Cummins engine and Voith transmission, has performed excellently since it was handed over officially at York Works. On 10 November the unit was photographed awaiting departure from Matlock with the 1500 service to Derby. *(John Tuffs)*

Below: On 30 November, the prototype Class 150 No 150001 was used for a demonstration run to Blackpool from Manchester Victoria for the benefit of Greater Manchester PTE officials and local councillors. The passengers had previously sampled the Class 141 on a ride to Marple. Blackpool's first sight of a 150 is shown here. *(Colin Boocock)*

Left: The second class 150, No 150002, a two-car unit, stayed in the shadows of No 150001, probably because more problems were encountered with it! This is the unit with Rolls Royce Eagle C6 280 HR engines driving Self Changing Gears R500 gearboxes and cardan shafts to the final drives. Both sets were tested on the Midland main line and ran coupled to St Pancras. By the year-end, No 150002 had not entered passenger service and was still under the scrutiny of the engineers. On 20 December it had a test run to Buxton from Manchester and these two views show the still experimental set at Stockport and pausing at Furness Vale. *(David N Clough; Steve Turner)*

Trans-Pennine dmu retirement

Above: The date of 13 May saw the end for arguably the finest looking dmus yet built in this country, the Class 124 'Trans-Pennine' units. With the exception of a short period allocated at Neville Hill, Leeds, the Class 124s were always based at Botanic Gardens depot, Hull. In 1979 the 'Trans-Pennines' ceased to be rostered to Manchester and Liverpool by their long-standing route via Leeds and Diggle and, instead, began working the 'South Trans-Pennine' route from Hull-Doncaster-Sheffield-Manchester and, occasionally, Liverpool. Another new working took two units to Morecambe from Leeds and this route continued to play host to these dmus until the end. Approaching Settle Junction is a Class 124 vehicle heading the 1342 Morecambe-Leeds on 24 March. *(Gavin Morrison)*

Left: Also rendered extinct on 13 May were the 'Trans-Pennine' interlopers, the Class 123 units which were drafted into the ER from the WR in 1977. This wintry reminder of the 123s on the 'South Trans-Pennine' route picture shows, nearest the camera, No E52096 leading the 1245 Manchester-Cleethorpes while on the right is No E52094 heading the 1014 Hull-Manchester. The trains are passing at Buxworth on 25 January. *Above:* Starting out of Manchester Piccadilly is a Class 123 leading the 1245 to Cleethorpes on 5 April. Sadly no 'Trans-Pennines' were preserved. The Moors Railway had intended to acquire a 3-car set but subsequent abandonment of the line's off-peak timetable for the 1985 season precluded the need for the purchase. All vehicles from the ten sets which remained at the final day, Sunday 13 May, were duly sent to Darnall, Sheffield for removal of engines and gearboxes and boarding up prior to being stabled in Tinsley Secondary Yard pending scrapping. *(Steve Turner; David N Clough)*

PTE paintings

Above: To mark ten years of the South Yorkshire PTE on 10 March, Lincoln-based Class 114 unit Nos E53045/E54005 was turned out in the Executive's colours by BREL Doncaster. Sheffield is the setting of this picture taken on 23 April. *(Les Nixon)*

Left: Greater Manchester was another PTE to exercise the livery prerogative when 25 kV ac unit No 303060, one of eight allocated to the Hadfield service from December, received this treatment at Wolverton. Before entering service on this re-energised line the 3-car set was inspected by PTE officials and local councillors at Manchester Piccadilly on 30 November. Cruelly, the unit became known as 'The Jaffa Cake' for reasons which will be obvious to devotees of that particular confection! On Christmas Eve No 303060 was busy at Dinting on a Hadfield service. *(Colin Boocock)*

Above: The prototype Class 140 spent the summer in Cornwall, where it underwent trials on various lines including the Looe branch in place of the usual Class 121 single-car unit. During its time in Cornwall it was maintained at Laira, Plymouth. Here the unit passes the closed Hackney Yard, Newton Abbot on 3 July en route from Derby to Laira and its summer season in the Duchy. *(Charles F Beatson)*

Below: The Verona green and cream livery adopted by the West Yorkshire PTE for its Class 141 units is shown to advantage in this study of a set waiting at Wrenthorpe Sidings on 2 June before working the 1715 Wakefield Westgate-Huddersfield. *(Peter M Marsh)*

Class 141 railbus comes into service

All twenty 2-car Class 141 sets were commissioned during 1984 but the Regional Mechanical & Electrical Engineer's staff and his Neville Hill depot engineers had their hands full as the year progressed. The class duly entered public service but considerable problems were experienced with the gearboxes. Spares, or lack of them, was another problem for the engineers and one set was taken out of service in December and shown as 'stored unserviceable' on the official records!

Right: Crew training began in March and this picture shows the first Class 141 to reach York. Set No 141003 had just arrived from Leeds, Neville Hill and immediately returned to Leeds. The training runs usually consisted of shuttle trips between Leeds and York or Leeds and Harrogate. The date of this picture is 30 January. *(Murray Brown)*

Below: Set No 141002 moves out of Leeds on a training run to Harrogate on 9 March. The first five sets were sent to Doncaster Works following the delivery of No 141006 to be repainted in the PTE's green and cream livery. The full diagrams were introduced with the October timetable change and required the use of fifteen of the nineteen sets available for service, the prototype unit not having been delivered. *(John S Whiteley)*

The first six Class 141s were delivered in the dark blue Barrow Corporation livery, a darker shade than Rail Blue. This is in itself an astonishing occurrence, for one telephone call could have elicited the paint specification for Rail Blue! The story goes that Leyland did not know the correct colour and painted it in the nearest blue they stocked! However, as the West Yorkshire Passenger Transport Executive were paying for the services which the 141s were to operate, the PTE duly requested that the sets be painted in its own colours of Verona Green and cream. Thus set No 141006 arrived at Neville Hill on 16 March in the new colours and was ceremonially handed over to the PTE on 19 March at a ceremony at Leeds at which BRB Chairman Bob Reid officiated. The picture shows the unit arriving for the ceremony. No 141006 had been painted and tested on the Midland main line in dark blue livery but returned to Derby Litchurch Lane Works for painting in the PTE colours. *(Gavin Morrison)*

Left: The first public service diagram for the Class 141 was implemented on April 18 on the Leeds to Goole route. On 18 June a set arrives at Castleford with a service from Knottingley to Leeds. *(Colin Keay)*

Below

Left: The prototype set, No 141001, remained at Derby Technical Centre for the whole of 1984. By the year-end it was the only one of the twenty sets to remain in the original dark blue livery. On 14 March the unit was photographed passing through Melton Mowbray on the Leicester-Peterborough line during a test run. The Class 141s were usually worked as far as Corby on this line before returning to Derby. *(John Tuffs)*

Right: During 1984, 141s were demonstrated to other PTEs, one unit being sent to Tyneside for this purpose and another to Manchester. On this latter occasion, it was exhibited in Manchester Piccadilly before taking Greater Manchester PTE officials and local councillors on a run to Marple, where the unit is featured. It returned to Manchester Victoria where passengers transferred to a Class 150 for a run to Blackpool. *(Colin Boocock)*

Merseyrail units retired

Above: Condemnation commenced in earnest during 1984 of the Class 503 Merseyrail units. This Class consists of LMS 1938-built sets and BR 1956-built units. By the year-end only 1956-built sets were still in use, although two LMS 1938 units had been put to one side at Birkenhead Central carriage sidings for use on the final specials planned for 29 March 1985. This is LMS unit No M28677 + M29707 + M29276 leading a sister unit at Rock Ferry with a West Kirby service on 28 January. *(Steve Turner)*

Above: This 1956-built unit (M28383 + M29840 + M29150) leading a sister set into the ex-Mersey Railway station at Green Lane was one of those withdrawn during 1984. It is seen on 20 June on a Rock Ferry-Liverpool Central working. *(Colin Boocock)*

Right: These two 1956-built units survived to the year-end as part of the fleet of twelve such sets, but their time was running out. They are pictured at West Kirby on 1 December. *(Peter M Marsh)*

Class 506 finale

Top: BR's second oldest passenger stock, the Manchester - Hadfield Class 506 emus, came to the end of their lives after a 30-year reign. This left the Merseyrail Class 503 emus holding the title of oldest trains in regular service, excluding the IoW tube stock! The eight sets survived intact until the end of 1983 when fire damaged one and a hybrid unit was formed. In the closing weeks of the Class 506s' service, vehicles from set 1 and 2 were amalgamated to form another hybrid. This time-honoured scene at Guide Bridge shows unit No 2 on the 1745 Manchester - Hadfield (right) and No 6 on the Hadfield - Manchester on 7 June. The 1500V dc system gave way to the standard 25kV on the weekend of 8/9 December when a bus service was substituted prior to the Class 303s taking over. The opportunity was also taken to rationalise Guide Bridge by routing trains through the far platforms in the photograph shortly before the changeover date and abandoning the platforms which are occupied by these units here. *(Colin Boocock)*

Centre and below: There was undoubtedly some affection by locals for these old units and they possessed their own period charm. With the passing of these units into history, the control room still situated at Penistone and isolated from the surviving 1500V dc lines at Manchester closed on the evening of 7 December. Thus came an end to 1500V operation on BR. Savour the memories with these two views. The hybrid set No 8 approaches Manchester Piccadilly from Glossop on 8 June and set No 7 with pantograph at full stretch enters Glossop with the 1113 Hadfield to Manchester on 4 December. *(Gavin Morrison; John Tuffs)*

Left: BR agreed to run a special on 17 November which included a non-stop run over the 1500V dc route. This was the last full Saturday of Class 506 operation, for the subsequent weekends included part bus and dmu service while the route was prepared for conversion. Sets Nos 4 and 8 formed the special, which is pictured at Dinting during a photo-call. *(Peter M Marsh)*

Below: The end of an era. Friday evening, 7 December and sets Nos 4 and 2, the latter a hybrid of 1 and 2, are seen about to depart from Glossop on the final train, the 1858 Hadfield-Manchester. Because of the nature of the service – an out and home working – the rare opportunity was present to place the customary detonators on the tracks for both outward and return journeys. The final train arrived at Piccadilly station amid continuous blowing of its horn and a welcome by a huge crowd. *(Steve Turner)*

Right: The Class 506 Group was formed in the autumn to raise funds for the preservation of a 506. When it became known that the West Yorkshire Transport Museum based on the Spen Valley line were also interested in obtaining a Class 506 set, the two concerns sensibly decided to combine resources. After extensive inspections and guidance by BR engineers, Set No 4 was nominated as being the best one for a preservation attempt. As the year ended, this unit had been put to one side away from the remaining sets stored outside Piccadilly and stabled at the Dinting Railway Centre. This picture is dated 24 December. *(Colin Boocock)*

Top: In 1984 the first refurbished examples of the good-looking Class 303 emus were turned out of BREL's Glasgow Works. Clas 303 No 303056, life-extended and refurbished, stands in Shields depot on 25 June. Set 056 is one of the later units already fitted with independent window frames (thus reducing body corrosion) and therefore did not receive hopper windows. The units to receive hopper windows are Nos 001-34. *(Colin Boocock)*

Centre: The interior of refurbished unit No 303056. Side walls are dove grey, end walls and cross-vestibules primrose yellow. Loose seat covers (standard with Class 314) are bright blue striped. The effect is dazzling! Set No 303006 was the first to be refurbished and it also carries the Glasgow PTE colours first unveiled in 1983. It was handed over by Scottish General Manager Chris Green to Councillor Malcolm Waugh, Chairman of the Strathclyde Regional Council Highways & Transportation Committee at a ceremony in Glasgow Central station on 6 June. *(Colin Boocock)*

Below: One of the refurbished Class 303 units fitted with hopper windows is seen at Glasgow Central on 19 September. It is No 303014 and was forming the 1255 Glasgow-Gourock service. *(Colin Boocock)*

Above: A new service to play host to the 24-year old Class 303s was the re-energised Manchester-Hadfield line, which saw its first 303s on the morning of 10 December. Making history is unit No 303036 which formed the first 25kV service from Glossop on the morning of the new service. The train is the 0619 to Manchester. *(I M Bradbury)*

Left: A total of eight Class 303s were dedicated to the Hadfield line services when they commenced operation on 10 December. This view shows unit No 303060, repainted in Greater Manchester PTE colours, rounding the corner at Dinting crossing on a Hadfield-Glossop-Manchester working on Christmas Eve. *(Colin Boocock)*

Below: Twelve Class 304 units were reduced to 3-car formations to cope with the Class 303 timings on the Liverpool-Crewe run when the 303s were transferred to the Manchester-Hadfield-Glossop service from 10 December. This picture shows 3-car Class 304 set No 304045 at Manchester Piccadilly on 10 November. The sets affected by reduced formations were, at the year end, Nos 304008/32-7/9-41/3/5. *(Colin Boocock)*

APT comes good

Above: 1984 was the year when the APT vindicated itself and ran many thousands of miles, in the process gaining a hitherto unheard of reputation for reliability. Passenger comfort tests continued in the early part of the year to evaluate stress and the level of tilt which could comfortably be undertaken before the ride became unpleasant for passengers. One such run is illustrated here as Nos 370007 and 370008 negotiate Low Gill while returning to Carlisle from Preston on 6 April. *(Peter J Robinson)*

Below: A contestant for 1984's most astonishing spectacle was the sight of an APT travelling at 100 mph on the East Coast Main Line . . . and remember, there are no overhead wires installed yet! This remarkable story started on 16 July and continued for just under three weeks. Two APT sets were towed to Heaton to participate in drag resistance tests between Darlington and York. Three return trips were scheduled and these took place in the early hours. During these runs the APT was propelled up to 100 mph by two modified Class 37s and released to verify how far it would coast. At the conclusion of each day's trials, the two Class 37s would couple to the APT at Northallerton and propel the vehicles to Eaglescliffe. Here the 37s would run round and haul the set via Darlington back to Heaton. This photograph depicts the APT being hauled back to Heaton at 0847 on the morning of 28 July. *(Peter J Robinson)*

Left: To test the principal of double-bogie tilting coaches, an APT vehicle was fitted with two separate bogies in 1984. No 48204 is seen at Crewe formed in the development train on 8 August. As the year progressed, plans were evaluated for the next generation of APT using some of the successful ideas gleaned from the prototype. The new train coined the name 'IC225', the figure denoting kilometres per hour (as another hallowed British way of life – miles per hour – bites the dust) and as the year ended, indications were that the IC225 would comprise tilting coaches propelled/pulled by a non-tilting electric locomotive likely to be designated Class 91. *(Colin Boocôck)*

Above: The APT was also put into passenger revenue earning service in the latter part of the year, being rostered as a relief service to scheduled trains. This picture shows sets No 370007 passing Leyland on 15 August. *(Les Nixon)*

Left: It is just after 2027 on 12 December as APT set No 370007 arrives at Glasgow Central having clinched the speed record for the journey from London Euston. BR's bid for the record began at 1635 when with no advance publicity the train set out on the 401-mile journey. Running at an average speed of 103 mph, the APT took just 3 hrs 52 mins to reach Glasgow, and this performance included 5 mins lost at Stafford due to a track circuit failure. Delighted BR officials greeted this achievement as vindication of their patient persistence with the tilting train principle and foresaw a new generation of such vehicles on the West Coast route behind the projected new Class 91 locomotives. *(BR, Glasgow)*

SR loses 508s

Opposite
Top: Continuing deliveries of Class 455 emus allowed the SR to say farewell to its Class 508s in 1984, with no sets rostered for use after 7 December. During the autumn the remaining sets still not sent to Merseyside had their formations reduced, thus allowing the spare TS (trailer second) cars to go to York Works for modification and subsequent insertion in new Class 455 units. 3-car Class 508s Nos 508036 and 508024 depart from Wimbledon with the 1012 Waterloo-Dorking on 25 September. The Class 508 had spent five years on the SR. *(Colin J Marsden)*

Below: Transfers of Southern Region Class 508 units to the LMR's Merseyrail system continued throughout 1984. Nos 508034 with 508028 bringing up the rear formed the 1143 Effingham Junction to Waterloo on 10 July. It is branching round towards Bookham. Set No 028 is a 3-vehicle set, having already yielded one trailer which, along with other trailers removed from sister sets, was sent to York Works for subsequent insertion in the new Class 455 units. *(Chris J Wilson)*

This page
Above: Class 508 units in Birkenhead North workshop in the early (set 508016) and final (set 508123) stages of conversion to fit the Liverpool area network. To avoid confusion with the similarly numbered Class 507 units the 508s were renumbered in the 101XX series, starting with No 508123, which had been renumbered half an hour before this picture was taken on 6 June. *(Colin Boocock)*

Left: Although the Class 508 had been used for some months on the Northern line, ex-SR 508s made their debut on the Wirral line in June 1984. Here unit No 508123 enters West Kirby on 26 June with the 0801 from New Brighton. *(Fred Kerr)*

Right: When the Class 501 units are withdrawn from Watford - Euston/Broad Street in May 1985, the intention is to replace them with surplus Class 313 units from the GN. To this end unit No 313006 was modified with extra shoe gear and undertook tests on the lines used by the Class 501s. The unit is seen stabled on Willesden depot on 12 November, four days after arriving for tests. Some difficulties were encountered with the shoe gear fouling obstructions. A total of 17 units are likely to be required in place of the Class 501s and Class 313 units Nos 313001-17 have been nominated to cover this service. Maintenance will continue to be undertaken at the units' home depot of Hornsey. *(Murray Brown)*

Below: Strangers in paradise? Well, not quite paradise, for this is Broad Street, the station BR would like to close. EPB units Nos 6309 and 5773 offer an unusual sight while undertaking gap tests on 6 June. *(Colin J Marsden)*

Above: On 6 and 7 June Southern Region 2EPB units No 6309 and 5773 operated a series of special runs to test the conductor rail gaps on the Richmond-Broad Street and the Euston-Watford routes. These tests were a prelude to 2EPB units taking over on the North Woolwich-Richmond line (and into Broad Street while it is still open), scheduled for 1985. Following the successful conclusion of these tests, 2EPB units Nos 6301-21/23 were nominated for this service, for which they will be fitted with barred windows in view of the limited clearances in Hampstead tunnel. Here the two EPB units approach Willesden on 6 June while en route from Broad Street to Watford via Primrose Hill. *(Colin J Marsden)*

North London emu replacements

GE emu changes

Above: From the May timetable, Class 315 units began work on the Lea Valley and Chingford routes. Modifications were necessary to provide a vehicle capable of being locked for parcels traffic. In this picture, No 315823 leaves Broxbourne on 30 May with a mid-day Hertford East-Liverpool Street working. *(Peter Groom)*

Below: Deemed surplus to requirements, two of the Class 308 4-car luggage units, Nos 308991 and 308992, were condemned and sent for storage at March and subsequent disposal in 1984. One of the vehicles, the power car from No 308991, was retained at Ilford as a store vehicle for seats. Pictured at March amid other withdrawn stock is unit No 308992. The Class 37 is not condemned! For the record it is No 37263 and was photographed on 30 September. *(Ian Cowley)*

Ayr fire drama

Left: A disastrous fire at Ayr depot on 3 January 1984 resulted in several dmu vehicles being wrecked and had repercussions on services and dmu formations for many months. Here is the scene of the occurrence with burnt vehicles shunted out after the fire. *(Colin Boocock)*

Right: Various LMR and ER dmu sets were drafted in to help the Scottish Region cope with the aftermath of the Ayr fire and the ScR quickly put set numbers on the transferred LMR Birmingham Class 104s. This picture shows numbers being applied to set No 104451 under the quickly repaired Ayr depot shed roof in January. *(Colin Boocock)*

Below: For many weeks hybrid formations could be seen in Scotland as a result of the conflagration at Ayr. Illustrating this phenomenum is this unusual formation sitting in Glasgow Central: an ER Class 101 Metro-train twin turned into a triple by the insertion of a LMR Class 104 power car. This scene is dated January 1984. *(Colin Boocock)*

Below: Those LMR vehicles transferred officially were subsequently put through Glasgow Works and repainted in blue and grey livery. Set No 104450 makes a fine sight passing Elderslie on the 1445 Ayr-Glasgow Central on 26 May. On the left can be seen the last Glasgow & South Western Railway signal which was later abolished under the Ayrshire resignalling scheme. The question is who pinched the finial since last year's *Jane's Railway Year?* *(Mrs Mary Boocock)*

LMR dmu miscellany

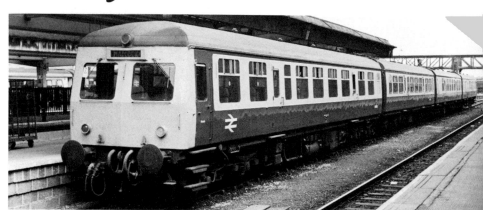

SR emu changes

Left: With the South Western commuter service largely in the hands of the new Class 455s by December, withdrawal took place in the same month of the 15 ex-Tyneside 2-EPB units. These were numbered in the range 5781-5795 but, like their earlier-numbered sisters from 5702 onwards, they were renumbered in the 62XX series to avoid clashing with the 455s which were replacing them. So, it's goodbye from him to the former Geordie units with this picture of unit No 6285 which had just been renumbered from No 5785. It was leading a formation of the 1704 Waterloo - Shepperton when photographed leaving Wimbledon on 13 August. *(David Brown)*

Centre: The fleet of 24 4CAP units was transferred from the Central Division to the South Eastern Division *en bloc* with the inauguration of the Gatwick Express service. This may sound a strange statement but it was a 'cascade' effect, for the Class 73/1s and Mk 2s replaced the 4VEG units (renumbered and reclassified to VEP units) which were duly rostered on the Coastway service and other Central Division duties in turn, ousting the 4CAPs. Here is a view of the Class 413/2 4CAP units in their new habitat: Nos 3212 and 3201 form the 1536 Margate-Victoria on 23 July at Bickley Junction. *(Brian Morrison)*

Bottom: With the introduction of the dedicated Gatwick Express trains on 10 May, there was no longer any requirement for the Class 427 4VEG units which hitherto had been used for this service. The 4VEG units were modified Class 423 4VEP units with extra luggage space and carried the numbers 7901-7912. After the Gatwick Express introduction, they were returned to their original classification and numbers (7788-7799), although internally they retained their extra luggage space. In this picture ex 4VEG No 7903, now 4VEP No 7790 rolls along the Mid-Sussex line near Amberley with the 1238 Victoria - Littlehampton on 29 May. *(Chris J Wilson)*

455 update

Above: Delivery of the 74 4-car units forming the first series of Class 455 (Nos 5801-5874) was completed during 1984. All went to the South Western Division to work suburban services out of Waterloo, including the Waterloo-Guildford via Effingham Junction route. No 5849 was experimentally given roof-level unit numbers during the year in an attempt to improve their legibility, the standard position for set numbers being tucked away behind the jumper cables! This unit was photographed at Wimbledon on an Epsom service on 17 June. *(Alex Dasi-Sutton)*

Below: During 1984 21 examples of the second batch of Class 455s with the revised front end entered service, also on Waterloo suburban services. An 8-car formation of Nos 5702 and 5704 approaches Wimbledon on 28 September with the 1105 Chessington-Waterloo. These 455s contain the trailer car removed from the 4-car Class 508 unis before the latter moved to Merseyrail. The third vehicle in each set is the former 508 vehicle, clearly discernable by the roof and body profile. *(Colin J Marsden)*

Wight celebration

On 28 January, car No S43 on the Isle of Wight (ex-LT-7275) celebrated 60 years in passenger service, first running on the Hampstead & City Line of the London Underground. The Electric Railway Society, London Underground Railway Society and the Southern Electric Group organised the celebrations which included Ryde depot opening to the public for the first time. The special train which included S43 carried a headboard at each end in the form of the LT bullseye sign and the BR emblem combined. The special is pictured at Ryde Esplanade and No S43, repainted for its birthday, at Ryde St John's Road. *(Both: Brian Hardy)*

BR COACHING STOCK

Mk 1s refurbished

One of the delights of 1984 was the emergence from Derby Litchurch Lane Works of the first Mk 1 coaches to be refurbished. This initiative came from InterCity Director Cyril Bleasdale, who authorised the scheme on twelve vehicles (two rakes of six) at a time when there was a lull in the Mk 3 coach build. Such was the speed at which the idea was formulated that no official estimates were prepared for the work. 100 mph dual-heated vehicles were nominated and the work entailed the removal of the steam-heating, external painting into Executive livery and bright new interiors. BREL also refurbished one SK vehicle, No M18753, with six-a-side seating. The twelve coaches were TSOs Nos M4919/27/30/46/61/66/79/96/5001/8 and BSKs Nos M35454 and M35465. The pictures show the external and internal views of TSO vehicles. One is left pondering why this simple, effective and inexpensive refurbishment was not contemplated years ago in view of the fact that the later build Mk 1 bodies are still sound and fit for many years service. Provincial Services Sector please note! *(BREL)*

What's in a name

Top: If it moves, ScotRail it! This was the message north of the Border in 1984. However, things did seem to have gone a little beserk with examples of non-standard lettering. Here are a few of the anomalies. The mixture of 'Inter-City' and 'Scotrail' legends as shown on the DBSO of the 0800 from Edinburgh after arrival at Glasgow Queen Street on 19 September was not the original intention. (Although the Edinburgh-Glasgow shuttle links Scotland's two principal cities they are not part of Mr Bleasdale's InterCity business sector.)

Right: The Scotrail logo was not intended to be used on catering cars either but was applied to RBR No SC1663, pictured at Preston in the 1120 'European' from Glasgow to Harwich on 2 April.

Above and right: With 'Trans-Clyde', 'Scotrail' and a 'terrier' on DMU No SC51464, is there room for anything else? The coolant filler connection looks in need of some lettering! The dmu was photographed at Queen Street, Glasgow on 15 October. Finally, it was thought a capital 'R' was needed in the Scotrail name so as to stop people misreading it as Sco-trail! How do you spell 'pathetic'? This TSO shows the final (?) version of ScotRail in Queen Street station on 15 November.
(All: *Colin Boocock*)

Right: As the overnight trains from Glasgow and Inverness came to rest at Inverness and Glasgow respectively at breakfast time on Monday May 14, the 27-year reign of the BR Mk 1 sleeping car came to an end. Only seven vehicles remained in use at the turn of the year and this pool was utilised on the above mentioned Scottish internal services only. Several Mk 1s have been obtained by preservationists, despite the blue asbestos content, and BR retained several for temporary Departmental use following their demise from revenue-earning service. The final trains to include Mk 1 sleepers were the 2350 from Inverness and the 2330 from Glasgow headed by Nos 47595 and 47610 respectively. The latter is pictured before departure at Queen Street, Glasgow with SLC No 2423 providing the sleeping accommodation. The next night Mk 3 vehicles took over. *(Colin Boocock)*

Stock changes in the Highlands

Above: For the Fridays-only 'Jacobite' 1303 Edinburgh (not Glasgow in 1984) to Inverness, the Scottish Region provided their Mk 2 Push-Pull set, here propelled by Class 47/7 No 47702 *Saint Cuthbert*, dropping down between Tomatin and Moy on 20 July. *(Colin Boocock)*

Left: To enable it to run air-braked day stock with Mk 3 sleeping cars to Fort William, the Scottish Region had four Mk 1 TSOs converted from vacuum to dual brakes. Two of these lead the formation behind Class 37 No 37018 and ETHEL 3 on the 0550 Glasgow-Fort William on 28 May. The sleepers are at the back. The formation includes Mk 1, Mk 2 pressure-ventilated and Mk 2 air-conditioned and Mk 3 stock. The only item missing is a Freightliner vehicle (see page 121)! *(Mary Boocock)*

61

Brake embellishments

Above: The first Mk 1 vehicles to carry the InterCity Executive livery appeared in 1984. This NEA No M92146 was in the formation of the 1145 to Glasgow pictured at Euston on 11 December. This train was not one the four 110 mph services despite the vehicle being stencilled to work at this speed. *(Colin Boocock)*

Below: The Eastern Region painted white stripes (strictly taboo at Eastfield!) on the BG vehicles dedicated to the Anglo-Scottish overnight trains to identify them as circuit-worked vehicles. NDX No E80914 is seen at Glasgow Queen Street on 15 October. This painting was a little surprising in view of the fact that vehicle movements are monitored by the Regional Operations Manager, notwithstanding the impending placing of coaching stock vehicles on the TOPS computer system (a trial system was inaugurated in East Anglia in the autumn of 1984), which will readily identify the whereabouts of all rolling stock. *(Colin Boocock)*

Shipshape stock

Above: 1984 saw the operation of the complete rakes of reliveried 'Sealink' vehicles on the Stranraer line. Ironically, Sealink changed its colours prior to being put on the market as part of the government's privatisation policy and thus the Stranraer livery became outdated as soon as it was inaugurated. Beauty is in the eye of the beholder, so the saying goes, and you must make up your own mind from this view of Class 47 No 47371 approaching Irvine on 24 July. *(Tom Noble)*

Below: The startling livery for the Glasgow to Stranraer boat trains was modified from the prototype – see *JRY* 1983 – to match more closely the Northern Ireland Railways example. This photograph shows the first two production vehicles in red, three shades of blue and white at Cowlairs in February 1984. The vehicles were also facelifted with the addition of fluorescent lights, yellow vestibules and inside door faces. System maps were also provided. *(Colin Boocock)*

Leicester asbestos plant opens

Above: A notable development in coaching stock disposal took place early in 1984 with the commissioning of a new blue asbestos disposal plant operated by the firm of Vic Berry of Leicester. This was particularly significant to BR as it provided a second outlet for scrapping contaminated stock to the one contractor who previously had the sole facilities for dealing with such vehicles, Mayer Newman at Snailwell. While the ER Mechanical & Electrical Engineer's department was responsible for moving vehicles to Snailwell from Tinsley Secondary Yard, the LMR catered for vehicles bound for Leicester and, during the year, sleepers from Tinsley, EMUs from the Southern Region and DMUs from the LMR were processed by Vic Berry. This view shows one of the rakes of Mk 1 sleepers en route from Tinsley to Leicester headed by Class 37 No 37251 at Cossington on 8 August. *(Paul A Biggs)*

Left: One of 1984's most unusual railway sights was provided at Vic Berry's yard. As B5 bogies were wanted urgently by BR for refurbishment schemes, there was a need to feed sleepers into Berry's yard quickly so that the bogies could be recovered and sent to Stanway, Colchester for assessment. Thus the spectacle was provided of three-tier coaches giving a new meaning to the phrase stacking sleepers! SLS vehicles and catering cars were piled high on the date of this picture, 28 October. *(Dennis Taylor)*

Below: With only one outlet for blue asbestos vehicles until Vic Berry gained the necessary licences, the Regions had inevitably to store vehicles for many months until they could be hauled to Snailwell, during which time more vehicles had been condemned, adding to the problem. With the opening of the Leicester plant, inroads were made into long-condemned vehicles as shown in this view of Park Royal Class 103 No M50403 seen being dismantled on 29 September. This vehicle had been condemned at Chester and stored at Carlisle. *(Steve Knight)*

Following the successful operation of observation saloons on the Mallaig branch in 1983, a saloon was procured for use on the Oban line for the 1984 season. It was the 1942-built LMS vehicle ADM 45030 which, commendably, was repainted in LMS livery but with yellow ends and numbered 45030. Its roster was the 0820 Glasgow-Oban and 1500 return and it ran Mondays to Fridays from the end of May until the end of September. A supplementary charge of £2 was levied. This picture shows Scottish initiative at work on the rear of the 0820 from Glasgow passing Cowlairs Junction on 4 September. *(Tom Noble)*

Saloon innovations

The observation saloon used on the Fort William to Mallaig services in the summer of 1984 was the former LMR vehicle TODM999501, built in 1957. It is seen at Fort William sporting its West Highland terrier motif on 2 October after its spell of duty was over for the season. Apart from the fact that it is incorrectly numbered (it should be TDM prefix), it is most unorthodox to use Departmental vehicles for revenue-earning use without renumbering them in the correct range or by dropping the prefix – see 45030 above. The two former LNER saloons used on the Mallaig run in 1983, Nos DE 900581 and DE 902260, were sold in 1984 to Mr Bill McAlpine (without competitive tender) with the proviso that they could be leased by BR. Both vehicles required work and were moved to Carnforth for attention to be given. *(Tom Noble)*

BR AND PRIVATE-OWNER WAGONS

Above: Britain's first wagon built from wide aluminium extrusions entered traffic for Foster Yeomans in 1984. The use of aluminium allows a saving of 20-tonne in the tare weight on a 102-tonne glw wagon. The production batch built by Procor is numbered PR17801-17837 and coded PHA. Here PR17801 is seen during tests by the BR Research & Development Department, Derby. It is passing Colthrop on 10 July with former Hawksworth Auto trailer, now Test Car No 1, ADW 150375 and Class 47/0 No 47103. *(D E Canning)*

Right and below: 160 of these POA vehicles took to the rails in 1984. They are 51-tonne scrap wagons and are owned by Railease. Those numbered in the 5000-5099 range are conversions, while those numbered 5921-5980 are new build. Their role is to replace the ageing MCV and MXV types. A close-up of three POAs in McIntyres scrapyard, Beeston, Nottingham on 19 October shows three of these wagons. The size of the POAs can be gauged from the picture showing four heading north at Stapleford & Sandiacre behind Class 25 No 25251 on 22 November. *(Both: John Tuffs)*

Right: Several brand new builds of air-braked wagons were introduced during 1984. Here Hall Aggregates PHA No 13708 stands at Newhaven prior to being used on a new service between this point and Tolworth. The wagon was built by the Standard Wagon Company and is one of a batch of 13 numbered 13700-13712. The vehicle illustrated was delivered in October. *(Michael J Collins)*

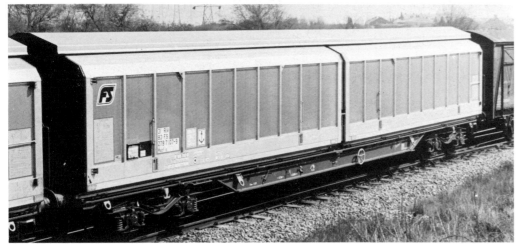

A sizeable portion of new wagons to be seen on BR are now built to RIV specifications for ferry operation and are Continentally registered. Not all these wagons are allocated to international traffic flows: some are used on internal services only. Three types to appear in traffic in 1984, all photographed at Hoo Junction, are illustrated here:

Left: 31.83.2979.107-9 is an Italian State Railways large capacity van. Its TOPS code is ILA and its livery is aluminium sides and roof, brown solebar and ends with black lettering on white. The photograph was taken in April 1984. *(R Wallace)*

Centre: The Transfesa Company owns this Spanish-registered van, No 24.71.2396.119-2, TOPS-coded ITX. Its livery is aluminium sides, blue end and black solebar and running gear. This picture was taken in November. *(R Wallace)*

Left: One of the most distinctive wagons to run on the BR system made its debut in 1984 when 30 of these PIA wagons were delivered (7 in July and 23 in October). They are owned by Storage & Transport System (STS) and are painted orange with 'STS' in black and red. French builder Fauvet Girel supplied them and this picture shows No 33.70.9382.103-7 in August, soon after delivery. *(R Wallace)*

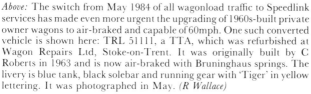

Above: The switch from May 1984 of all wagonload traffic to Speedlink services has made even more urgent the upgrading of 1960s-built private owner wagons to air-braked and capable of 60mph. One such converted vehicle is shown here: TRL 51111, a TTA, which was refurbished at Wagon Repairs Ltd, Stoke-on-Trent. It was originally built by C Roberts in 1963 and is now air-braked with Bruninghaus springs. The livery is blue tank, black solebar and running gear with 'Tiger' in yellow lettering. It was photographed in May. *(R Wallace)*

Above right: This is prototype Metalair tank wagon BCC 10988 and is a conversion from APCM 9142. It was completed by Powell Duffryn in February, is coded PCA and was pictured on 21 October at Hoo Junction. *(R Wallace)*

Right: A further eight tanks of the type illustrated here were delivered in January and February of 1984, completing the order. They are owned by Procor (UK) Ltd and the final eight are numbered 10125-10134. The picture shows No 10133 at Carlisle Kingmoor in July. *(Michael Rhodes)*

Below right: A number of changes have been made in BR's fleet of Runner wagons. The last of the vacuum-braked Runner wagons have been condemned. Pictured awaiting disposal at Temple Mills in February 1984 was RRV No B935890. *(R Wallace)*

Below: In order that more Departmental traffic could be transferred to Speedlink services, the transfer of revenue fleet air-braked wagons to Departmental fleets has continued, and there are few air-braked wagon types which do not have some representatives in Departmental usage. In this September 1984 picture, a YAA, No DC 950035, is seen at New Cross Gate, now in the Civil Engineer's fleet and known as a 'Brill'. Bogie Bolster Ds in the number ranges 950000-202/801-850 have also been transferred to Departmental service. *(R Wallace)*

Top: The return of the 'mixed' train between Aberdeen and Wick on 26 March (see p121) involved the use of four air-braked PJB container-carrying wagons. They were modified by having steam and vacuum through pipes so they could operate with vacuum-braked, steam-heated coaches and dual-braked locomotives. The containers carry general merchandise in conjunction with road haulage company Sutherlands Transport Ltd. Pictured at Aberdeen is FJB No 601998 on 27 March. It was converted from Freightliner inner wagon 602206 in 1977. *(R Wallace)*

Centre: 14 ex-CCT van underframes were converted by New Cross Gate C&W Department to London Regional Transport Adaptor wagons to replace elderly unfitted wagons. The number range is B902601-14. Here is No B902609, now designated a RFQ. It is used when underground stock is required to travel on BR tracks. Note the use of concrete sleepers as additional tare weight. The livery is freight brown. *(R Wallace)*

Below left: The vehicles for the 'Mercury' project were converted during 1984, the wagons at New Cross Gate and the coaches at Slade Green. The wagons for use on lines with overhead catenary have had a lightweight canopy fitted. This is KDB 923040, a YVW and is a former Bogie Bolster C, converted to a cable drum carrier with canopy and air through pipe. On this particular vehicle, the TOPS code is showing YNW incorrectly. The photograph was taken at Hoo Junction on 28 April. *(R Wallace)*

Bottom: 170 ex-Steel AB Runner wagons have been converted by BREL Doncaster and Derby to FPA (Conflat P) to carry containers of coal to Scotland. To replace these, 54 ex VQB Palvans that have been displaced from Ford traffic have had their bodywork removed and steel rails put on their floors to increase tare weight by Doncaster BREL and are coded RRB. The picture shows RRB No B787415 at Temple Mills in July 1984. One of the FPA wagons carrying a coal container, No 400178, is seen on 7 December at Doncaster, where it was being inspected by NCB officials. *(R Wallace; Colin J Marsden)*

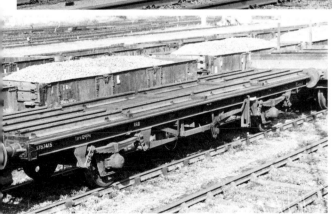

BR NETWORK

How did the BR network fare in 1984? It was indeed a mixture of good and bad which sometimes was hard to accept, with rationalisation evident everywhere in the shape of sidings and yards being pulled up and lines singled. Against this, in response to the acceptance by the government of BR's 1983 5-year corporate plan, authorisation was given for electrifying the Southminster branch, the Romford-Upminster branch, the North London line from Stratford to Willesden and the 'big one', the East Coast Main Line, although there was a sting in the tail with all of them, particularly the ECML project – BR has to foot the bill from its own resources. As this is to cost £306m, it is a poor reflection on how the country treats its national railway system, a far cry from the practice of European neighbours such as France and Belgium.

New developments included more stations opening as a result of financial backing from Regional, County or local Councils. One of BR's banes, the historic building, usually listed and requiring modernisation at vast cost, took an unusual twist with the announcement on 23 October that a Railway Heritage Trust was to be formed with an independent Chairman, the Rt Hon Bill McAlpine. The BRB was to put £1m into the venture.

One bright light – usually green – was the further extensions of power signalling as Three Bridges and Colchester extended their territory, and Westbury and Chester were commissioned. The days of the semaphore became numbered together with famous gantries which assumed far greater importance with the railway photographic fraternity.

There was also a positive outlook given to long-standing loss makers such as the Central Wales line and the Cambrian line when on 28 September BR announced plans for a £640 000 investment in the former and a £4.7m scheme to modernise the latter. However, one such line, the Settle & Carlisle, continued to be the subject of a tragi-comedy with BR having to issue the closure notices for a *third* time because they could not get the wording correct on the previously issued notices.

Below: Could this be the foretaste of things to come? The scene is Corby and the train, headed by Class 47/0 No 47146, is the first passenger train to call there since closure in 1966. It was organised by the Railway Development Society and ran from Kettering to Scarborough. Significantly Corby appears in BR's corporate plan as having a revival to the extent of being linked to the Midland Suburban Electrification scheme in association with the proposed Wonderworld project. Glendon Junction-Corby-Manton-Leicester is a freight route, avoiding the busy and heavily graded Kettering-Leicester direct line, though from Manton to Leicester, Peterborough line traffic joins and this includes passenger traffic. This picture is dated 1 July and shows the special arriving to pick up passengers. The single line track to BSC's tube works is on the left. This is the line used by the Lackenby-Corby 'Tubeliner' trains. (*J Checkley*)

Anglia prepares to go live

There was excellent progress during 1984 on the Anglia Electrification project. This scheme will involve an investment of nearly £100m over a five-year period. Plans went ahead on the new swing bridge at Trowse, Norwich to replace the existing structure, parts of which date back nearly 140 years. Meanwhile, masts sprouted along the route and by the year-end well over half of the 4300 required were in position. A third of the 300 km of overhead wire had also been erected. The following portfolio shows the transformation taking place on the Great Eastern main line which will bring Ipswich within 60 minutes of London.

Above: On 9 April the overhead wiring train was in action at Parsons Heath, east of Colchester, with No 31312 providing the power. *(Michael J Collins)*

Below: It may be better for the public and the operators, but electrification is not all roses. Environmentally, it is a blot on the landscape, although this is compensated for by the lack of diesel fumes. Brantham is the newly-wired location in this picture taken on 21 June as Class 47/4 No 47542 hurries along the 1017 Norwich-Liverpool Street. *(Peter J Robinson)*

Top left: Meanwhile, further east, the overhead line support foundation train was performing its duty between Haughley Junction and Stowmarket. On this day, 18 June, normal services were using the up line only. Power on this occasion was provided by Class 31 No 31246. *(Peter J Robinson)*

Left: During 1984 Ipswich saw major works involving resignalling, trackwork and refurbishment of the station itself. In this view track alterations are underway on 22 August as Class 47/4 No 47571 departs with the 1217 Norwich-Liverpool Street. Station improvements included the provision of a new travel centre and ticket office, modernisation of the toilets on platform 2, incorporating facilities for disabled people, and a clean-up for the station brickwork together with a total repaint. *(Hugh Ballantyne)*

Above: One of the major civil engineering projects in connection with the Anglia Electrification was the laying of slab track in Ipswich tunnel. Preliminary work commenced in April 1984 to replace the drainage system in the tunnel to improve conditions and installation of the slab track began in July. With the new signalling commissioned, it was possible to close one line whilst operating bi-directional trains over the remaining track. The down line was dealt with first and this picture shows the work in progress in its early stages as the trackbed is prepared. The photo is dated 15 July. Approaching is Class 47/4 No 47487 with an up London train. *(Ian Cowley)*

Below: The changing face of Belstead bank as the masts march forward. On 13 April the 0930 Liverpool Street-Norwich tops the summit behind Class 47/4 No 47579 *James Nightall GC*. *(Gavin Morrison)*

Above: Included in the Anglia scheme is the Harwich branch. This familiar sight on the GE in 1984, an electrification pw train on this this occasion headed by Class 37 Nos 37004 and 37057, was photographed passing Mistley on the Harwich branch on 13 April. *(Gavin Morrison)*

Above and right: Preparations continued in 1984 for the introduction of radio signalling on the East Suffolk line from Ipswich to Lowestoft. At the Ipswich end, as part of the resignalling, the junction at East Suffolk Junction was simplified and the signalbox abolished in October. Meanwhile, on the branch, traffic used the up line between Saxmundham and Melton while the down line was reballasted and refurbished. The down line then took all traffic and the up line between these points abandoned. Dmu services replaced the one existing locomotive hauled service – see **BR Traffic** section. Saxmundham will be the centre for the radio control and the total scheme is costing £1.2m. The new layout at East Suffolk Junction was photographed on 12 April with Class 31 No 31249 shunting ballast wagons. Another ballast train is seen at Saxmundham on 16 February behind Class 37 No 37075. *(Gavin Morrison; John A Day)*

Lichfield-Walsall closure

New West Midlands InterCity station

Right: Sandwell and Dudley was joined to the InterCity network on 14 May when BRB Chairman Bob Reid officially opened the new station buildings. *(Steve Knight)*

Below: Situated on the Birmingham to Wolverhampton line, Sandwell and Dudley was provided with an excellent service of main line and local trains. The station opened with a splendid piece of unplanned publicity – the first train sailed through without stopping! A general view of the station is provided with this view of Class 86/2 No 86232 *Harold Macmillan* arriving with the 1335 Manchester-Birmingham train on 4 October. *(Hugh Ballantyne)*

Right: The opening of Sandwell & Dudley station was accompanied by an unusual exhibition train in an unusual place. The somewhat derelict surroundings of Wolverhampton Low Level station was the setting for a condemned Class 25 No 25067 repainted for the occasion to be stabled together with a Mk 1 and two NFV brake vehicles. This station closed as a parcels concentration depot in 1981 and the remaining tracks were taken out of use in October 1984 pending removal. The station buildings on the down side will continue in use for office accommodation. The strange entourage is seen on 20 June. *(G F Bannister)*

Closure proposed

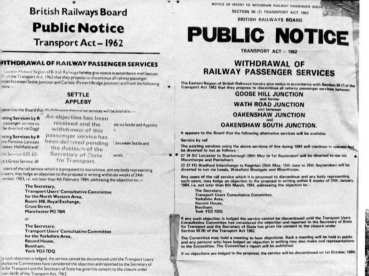
Above: The former Midland Railway Goose Hill Junction-Wath Road Junction section of line carried at one time the 'Thames-Clyde Express' and the 'Waverley'. It is now proposed for closure, all surviving freight services having been diverted from 1 October, leaving additionals or diverted trains as its sole traffic. Its demise can be blamed, ironically in this year under review, on mining, for subsidence brought about its fall from grace. In this view at Cudworth Station Junction on 13 February No 31301 leads condemned stock off the main MR route and down the Stairfoot Junction and Wath line. Being freight only, this particular link was closed without formality on 4 June. *(Les Nixon)*

Left: This photograph of two closure notices raises an interesting point in that both refer to main lines and, so we are told by BR and the politicians, it is not the intention to close such lines. It does appear that the small print in such matters allows BR to divert traffic from routes which thus renders the appellation of main line redundant and paves the way to closure. It really is not cricket, is it? Both notices refer to sections of the former Midland main line and were adorning a wall at Sheffield on 18 February. Objections, over 20 000 in the case of the S&C, were received, necessitating the convening of a public inquiry. *(Gary Grafton)*

Right: BR Eastern Region posted notices in June to the affect that it wished to close five sections of line traversed by holiday trains and occasional diverted traffic. These were: Wakefield Kirkgate-Hare Park Jct; Dryclough Jct-Greetland Jct; Milner Royd Jct-Heaton Lodge Jct; Bradley Wood-Bradley Jct; Horbury Station Jct-Crigglestone Jct.

As objections were received, the planned closure date of 1 October could not be implemented. One of the threatened lines is shown here as Class 47/4 No 47419 takes the single track at Bradley Junction, near Huddersfield, with the diverted 1155 York-Liverpool on 5 August. The train will joint the Calder Valley line at Milner Royd Junction. *(Stephen Willetts)*

Above: Although the Settle & Carlisle line proposal plan continued to make news in 1984 with its attendant huge list of official objectors, another line's supporters put up a tremendous fight and thus forced an inevitable delay to the proposed October closure date. The line was the Goole-Gilberdyke section of the Doncaster-Hull route. This picture shows the cause of BR's closure plans, the Goole swing bridge across the River Ouse. Its alleged poor condition reputedly with a repair price tag of £2m prompted BR to propose operating Goole at the end of the branches from Doncaster and Leeds and rerouting main line trains to and from Hull via Selby. It seems incredible that if a vessel damaged the bridge in an accident some years ago, BR is left to pay for repairs and not the shipping company involved. Here the infamous structure is being crossed by Class 31/4 No 31439 heading the 1513 Hull-Manchester on 18 September. *(David Farrar)*

Below: 1984 eth-converted No 31445 approaches Saltmarshe, the only station threatened with closure if BR succeeds in abandoning the Goole-Gilberdyke section. The 31/4 was heading the 1149 Hull-Manchester on 26 June 1984. *(Les Nixon)*

Coals to Newcastle

These two photographs show the major works which were necessary to reconnect rail lines to Tyne Dock Bottom to cater for a new coal export terminal. This terminal would receive coal trains mainly from the Sunderland area and a new east-north spur was to be laid at Pontop crossing at the top of the Tyne Dock incline, where the Sunderland-Newcastle line meets the Tyne Dock line. The planned inauguration date was January 1985 but the miners' dispute duly delayed proceedings. The pictures, taken on 26 December, show (*above*) the new terminal and the severed lines which led to Simonside wagon works, and (*left*) also the view looking south towards the formidable gradient up which once slogged the legendary Tyne Dock-Consett iron ore trains behind Class 9Fs. The bridge in the distance is new and the remains of the old water tower which serviced the steam traction is in the foreground. (Both: *Peter J Robinson*)

Consett line closure

Above: The Newcastle Division organised a farewell run to mark the closure of one of the most famous freight routes in the country – the line to Consett. Dereliction surrounded this line after the Consett iron works were closed. What is so sad is that there is potential for a revitalised passenger service to inject new life into the depressed Consett area. One such opportunity would have been an extension of the Metro system utilising the trackbed as far as Pontop crossing and joining up with the Heworth line. As the Metro cost £280m, however, with most of the finance being provided from central government, the prospect of an allocation of further millions is remote.

The Traction Maintenance Engineer at Gateshead specially provided Class 46 No 46026 *Leicestershire and Derbyshire Yeomanry* for the occasion and the 1115 Newcastle-Consett special provides a striking last look at the notorious 1 in 35 incline at Stanley on 17 March. *(Peter J Robinson)*

Below: This depressing scene is a reminder of how abolition of industry and economic factors can have such a devastating affect on railways, for this is the once busy Consett North Low Yard, with tracklifting underway on 15 August. *(L Abram)*

Scottish remodelling

Above, left and below: Extensive remodelling on a new alignment was put in hand at Dundee during the year in association with the resignalling scheme due for commissioning in 1985. The changing panorama is shown in these views illustrating Class 27 No 27032 arriving with the 1018 from Edinburgh on 20 September and the up 'Aberdonian', the 1000 Aberdeen-Kings Cross, leaving Dundee Tay Bridge on 19 October. In both views the new track alignment is under construction. Dundee signalbox displays a notice heralding the demise of the box when the resignalling is completed and adding that finance has been forthcoming from the European Regional Development Fund. *(Tom Noble; John A M Vaughan (2))*

Below: Class 37 No 37112 at Craigendoran Junction on Monday 5 November, the first day of operation of the new Craigendoran Junction signalbox. The train is the 0950 Glasgow-Fort William, which is joining the West Highland line by what was the former up line. The track in the right foreground is the down line, now out of use. The original layout can be discerned in the background. The secondman standing in the cab doorway is about to receive the token from the Craigendoran signalman, as token workings is still in operation between Craigendoran and Garelochhead. *(Tom Noble)*

Electrification preparations

On 27 July came an announcement that pleased some people and upset others. The Transport Minister, after stalling for six years, gave BR permission to electrify the East Coast Main Line to Edinburgh and the Doncaster-Leeds line at a cost of £306m. The part which angered many rail followers was the sting in the tail that the scheme was to be BR-funded. This did not surprise BR for it was known from the start that the cost of this electrification would have to be found internally. Initially the section from Hitchin to Huntingdon was to have been the first to be served by Class 317 emus but this plan was amended so that the first section to be re-equipped with electric trains would be Hitchin-Peterborough. May 1991 would see the full scheme implemented.

Visible work to be seen soon after the announcement was the establishment of an electrification depot at Peterborough Westwood Yard near the parcels terminal and the continuation of the bridge rebuilding schemes to permit the 25 kV wires to pass below. The first bridges to be rebuilt following the go-ahead were Nos 113 and 114 at Biggleswade, two of 164 which require remedial attention to allow the electrics to run from Hitchin to Leeds and Edinburgh. Tilbury Construction Ltd demolished the bridges over two weekends whilst main line trains were diverted via Cambridge. This picture of bridge No 113 shows the new deck being lifted into place on 25 November. *(Mervyn Askew)*

Laying of the third rails on the North Woolwich branch was completed by the autumn of 1984. The line was to be operated by Southern Region 2-EPB units from May 1985. The old order is illustrated by the old order literally! BR's oldest dmu class, the Cravens-built Class 105, provides the staple power on the branch. On 24 October a twin formed of Nos E53365 and E54421 calls at Stratford Low Level bound for Camden Road. The third rail spells the end for these units at Stratford depot. *(Michael J Collins)*

More new stations

Left and below: Auchinleck and Kilmaurs stations, situated on the Glasgow & South Western main line, were reopened on 12 May. Both were financed by Strathclyde Regional Council at a cost of £150 000 for Auchinleck and £90 000 for Kilmaurs. BR is to be commended with the speed with which the two stations were built. Auchinleck took just 16 weeks and Kilmaurs took only six weeks to construct. Both stations were originally closed under Dr Beeching's regime, Auchinleck on 6 December 1965 and Kilmaurs on 7 November 1966. The former is served by Glasgow-Carlisle trains while Kilmaurs is served by the hourly Glasgow-Kilmarnock dmus. The photographs show the two stations, Auchinleck viewed from a Euston-Glasgow relief on 29 June and Kilmaurs on 24 August as Class 27 No 27014 powers through on a Carlisle-Glasgow working. *(Colin Boocock; Tom Noble)*

British Railways Board

PUBLIC NOTICE
Transport Act 1962

RE-OPENING OF DYCE STATION

The BRITISH RAILWAYS BOARD hereby give notice, in accordance with section 56A of the Transport Act 1962, that, with effect from Saturday 15 September, 1984, they will re-open on an experimental basis their station at DYCE, GRAMPIAN REGION.

The Grampian Regional Council are contributing to the cost of the re-opening, the purpose of which is to find out whether, having regard to efficiency and economy, there is a sufficient demand for its use to justify permanent re-opening of the station.

GENERAL MANAGER,
SCOTTISH REGION,
BUCHANAN HOUSE,
58 PORT DUNDAS ROAD,
GLASGOW G4 0HG.

B14 - 02 84

When Dyce station was re-opened on 15 September, BR expected a useage of 70 000 passengers per year. By the end of the year it had been estimated that the figure would reach 180 000, due primarily to the excellent cooperation by the Grampian Regional Council, who tailored bus services to fit in with the train service and so avoid duplication. *(I C Scotchman)*

Right: Rail services came to the new town of Livingston for the first time on 6 October when Councillor Brian Meek, Convener of Lothian Regional Council, accompanied by BR Scottish General Manager Chris Green, unveiled a commemorative plaque at the new station of Livingston South to mark the official opening. Situated between Kirknewton and West Calder on the Edinburgh-Fauldhouse-Glasgow Central line, Livingstone South has cost £293 000 with associated works and has been financed by Lothian Regional Council and the Livingston Development Corporation. Improvements to services along this route have included doubling the train frequency to hourly and a special 50p fare valid until 27 October from Livingston South in each direction between Fauldhouse and intermediate stations to Edinburgh. Pictured entering the new station is a two-set Class 101 dmu special from Edinburgh carrying dignitaries for the official opening. Normal service trains began calling at Livingston South earlier on 6 October. On the right is the Inch House Pipe Band. *(Tom Noble)*

Above: Just another station opening? Yes, but with a difference, for it is not everyday that a station is moved down the line. This is South Bank station in the heart of industrial Teesside, which was officially opened on 14 May.

The unstaffed halt – all the stations on the Middlesbrough-Saltburn line became 'open' in 1984 – was resited from its previous position ¾-mile east, the old station being in need of repair and less suited to the changing domestic circumstances of the community. A Darlington-Saltburn service calls at the new station on 14 August. *(Peter J Robinson)*

Unlike West Yorkshire PTE, the South Yorkshire PTE has been a little backward in coming forward in opening new stations, preferring to concentrate most of its resources into providing unbelievably low bus fares. Rail finally got a look in in November when Silkstone Common station was re-opened on 28 November. This station is situated on the Penistone-Barnsley line, which is served by the Sheffield-Huddersfield dmu services. The station has cost £60 000 and South Yorkshire County Council decided to go-ahead with the scheme following the success of the rerouted Penistone-Sheffield trains via Barnsley where business had risen by 40% on closure of the direct route to Sheffield from Penistone in 1983. A twin Class 110 forming the 1108 Huddersfield-Sheffield calls at the unstaffed station on 28 December. *(Les Nixon)*

Above: Saltaire station opened for business on 9 April. It cost £139 000 and was officially opened by former railman Joe Moynihan, Vice-Chairman of West Yorkshire County Council. Saltaire residents have been without a station since 1965 when Dr Beeching axed the original facility and the new unstaffed station has 91 trains calling daily, as well as the Dalesrail specials. Saltaire was the sixth new station to be opened by the West Yorkshire PTE and worthy of mention is the provision of 'gas lamp' type electric lights which blend in so well. Less commendable is the pathetic saga of the West Yorkshire road planners. For years they have been suggesting routes for the Airedale trunk road to by-pass such places as Shipley, Baildon and Keighley and, incredibly, one new suggested route lies . . . you'll never guess where! It could only happen in England. This picture shows a Class 108 twin calling on the 1140 Skipton-Leeds. *(Les Nixon)*

Although Silkstone Common was in use from 26 November, it was not officially opened until 28 November. Here is the official 'Opening Day Special' comprising the reliveried dmu Nos E54004 and E53045 assisted in the rear by Metro-Cammell units Nos E53289 and E53272. *(Roger Milnes)*

Left: Following the diversion of Newcastle-Carlisle trains in 1982 from the Scotswood line north of the River Tyne to the Dunston line, calls came from the public, politicians and the NUR to reopen Dunston station, which closed as long ago as 4 May 1926 during the General Strike. The rebuilt station cost £100 000 and was funded jointly by BR, Gateshead Borough Council and a grant from the Department of the Environment. Gateshead Mayor Mrs Minnie Robson declared the station open on 1 October. Here, on the opening day, a dmu special which had made a return journey down the line to Prudhoe has just arrived back at Dunston. *(L Abram)*

Above and left: Lostock Hall station opened for business on 14 May. It is situated on the East Lancashire line between Farrington Curve Junction and Bamber Bridge and is served by 19 trains daily on the Preston-Colne route. The cost of £120 000 was borne by the Lancashire County Council. Since the original station closed 15 years ago, there has been a substantial increase in the local population. Here on the first day of operation the first train to use the station, the 0640 Preston-Colne, calls at the spotless platforms. A general view of the station is provided with the photograph depicting the 0943 from Colne and the 1038 from Preston pausing at Lostock Hall on 30 June. *(John Matthews; Les Nixon)*

Left: One of the strangest station reopenings took place in 1984 when passengers once again alighted at Sugar Loaf Summit platform, on the Central Wales line between Cynghordy and Llanwrtyd. Although never in public use, the halt was opened by the LNWR in 1899 and closed by BR in 1965. It served several railway families who lived in close proximity and never appeared in the public timetable. However, for four Saturdays (21 and 28 July, and 18 and 25 August) the platform was opened to cater for passengers taking part in an organised walk to Llanwrtyd Wells using the 1011 dmu from Swansea. The platforms are seen being passed by a Kidderminster-Tenby ADEX behind Class 25 Nos 25282 and 25279 on 1 August. *(Andrew Bannister)*

Signalling round-up

Continued progress in the programme of resignalling and rationalisation schemes during 1984 resulted in the total number of signalboxes in use on BR falling below the 2000 mark, from 2070 at the start of the year to 1960 at the close. Indeed, for some years the abolition of signalboxes has remained at just over 100 per year, but with the introduction of radio signalling and the extension of power box schemes, this figure is likely to increase. The year also saw an increase in the replacement of early power installations, reflecting how the years are passing. For example, two panel schemes at Ashburys and Guide Bridge replaced nine electro-pneumatic frames dating from Great Central Railway days some eighty years ago and the large 3-section power frame at Waterloo, installed by the Southern Railway in 1936, was replaced by a push-button panel in February.

Above: The number of traditional mechanical and electro-mechanical signalboxes in use on BR is rapidly declining, with over 100 examples being abolished during the year under review. Two of these are illustrated here: Chester No 6, closed during May, its functions being taken over by the new Chester powerbox; and Brighton Upper Goods, closed in June as part of the advance stage-work which is currently being undertaken in preparation for the whole of the Brighton area being controlled from Three Bridges by early 1985. *(David Wilkinson)*

Left: The once busy terminus at Bradford Forster Square was reduced to a pitiful remnant of former glories in September and October when the 1890-built Midland Railway 80-lever signalbox was abolished and the track layout reduced to the absolute bare minimum, with signalling controlled from Shipley (Bradford Junction). The box at Manningham Lane was also a casualty. In this view, the 0930 service from Ilkley formed of a Class 108 (Nos E54195 and E53620) arrives at Forster Square on 29 September. On the right stood the sidings in which were stored the withdrawn Class 306 units which were moved from here to Tinsley in the spring. *(Paul D Shannon)*

Left: In October the Westbury power box took over control of the West of England main line from Westbury to Bruton. One of the manual boxes to close was at Clink Road Junction, seen here as No 56031 *Merehead* comes up the Frome avoiding line with stone from the Yeoman quarry on 18 April. *(Les Nixon)*

The external construction of Exeter power box was completed in the year and installation of equipment proceeded with a view to commissioning the box in 1985. Work was at an advanced state in this picture dated 5 August. *(Roger Penny)*

An interior view of Exeter powerbox taken on 10 December. Route setting buttons are on the desks whilst the illuminated diagram showing the position of trains is on the rear wall. The two television screens on the centre rear desk are for control by closed circuit television (CCTV) of the level crossings at Exeter St Davids and Stoke Canon. *(David Wilkinson)*

Left: The rapidly changing panorama at Exeter. This December 1984 view was taken looking east with the 0725 Paddington-Penzance arriving. Exeter middle signalbox can be seen in the background. *(David Wilkinson)*

Below: A general view of the newly constructed Leicester power box which is at the heart of the £15m Leicester resignalling scheme to be commissioned in stages over the next three years. Completion of this project will bring about the abolition of semaphore signalling on the Midland main line. *(David Wilkinson)*

Above: Graphically portraying the fate which is now inevitable for so much semaphore equipment is this picture taken at Spalding on 21 July. A Class 37 sits on an engineers' train while the former up signal controlling the 'Joint' line to March and Boston is felled. Work which commenced on 13 May involved the reduction of platforms at this station to just two, the abolition of No 2 signalbox and a new panel commissioned in No 1 box. The work was completed on 22 July. (*John Rudd*)

Above: One of the most famous signals in the country, the magnificent North Eastern Railway slotted post signal at Haxby (up distant) on the Scarborough-York line was felled on 7 October. It was without doubt the largest intact signal of its kind and had become a favourite with photographers in recent years. Although its days were numbered (the Regional S&T Engineer had plans to replace it within the next three years), the decision was taken to exhibit this vintage signal in the concourse of York station following the £1m renovation scheme which included the provision of a travel centre. This picture shows the final train to pass the signal on 7 October. As the spectacle is lowered by the S&T technicians, the 1040 Scarborough-York emu passes by. (*Peter L Such*)

Right: The changing face of Scarborough is shown in these two pictures. Rationalisation came to this resort in the autumn when Falsgrave signalbox situated at the end of the platforms took over the whole of the station workings and Scarborough signalbox was abolished, together with the well known gantry. Shortly before the demolition men moved in, Class 46 No 46035 waits to leave with the 1410 Scarborough-Nottingham on 1 September. As the next picture shows, transformation was almost total with the locomotive being withdrawn, the signals and box being dispensed with and even the station not exempt, for the lines to the right of the photograph were taken up to allow the building of, yes, you've guessed, a supermarket. Nearly two months later, on 24 October, Class 45/1 No 45101 waits to leave with a Scarborough-Llandudno working whilst Class 37 No 37163 powers an engineering train being used to lift redundant track. (*D B Stacey; Michael Rhodes*)

Class 37 No 37025 accelerates away from Inverness with the 0625 to Wick on 12 May. The signals in this picture are now on numbered days following the announcement of a £3m resignalling scheme to be based at the Highland capital. *(John Whitehouse)*

Below: On 8 June **BRB** Chairman Bob Reid officially opened a £1.5m Service Centre for the Signal & Telecommunications Department at York station. It is situated on the west side of the station in an area formerly occupied by sidings. The new centre is one of three (the others being situated at Crewe and Wimbledon) which replaced seven old centres. The present workshops for the S&T at Toft Green York, were closed with the opening of the new building. A rail siding caters for the stores van services which use the Speedlink network. This internal view is of the Electro-mechanical Shop with, in the foreground, booms under construction for modernisation of level crossings. *(BR York)*

Above: Wheels always turn full circle and the railway wheel is no exception. On the Far North line all distant signals between Invergordon and Georgemas Junction were removed and replaced with reflectorised distant boards, such as this example south of Brora, pictured in July 1984. These boards were erected in the spring and involved north and south signals at Invergordon, Tain, Ardgay, Lairg, Rogart, Helmsdale, Forsinard and Georgemas Junction. But when did reflectorised boards last light-up? It was some 30 years ago on a long closed branch in north Yorkshire when lineside boards were installed on the Knaresborough to Boroughbridge branch and certain nominated steam locomotives were fitted with a headlight. At that time the idea was not considered successful. *(Tom Noble)*

The first fibre-optic banner signals, in place of conventional electro-mechanical banners, were installed during 1984. This example is at Wolverhampton, seen on 18 April. *(BR Derby)*

End of an era on the Kyle line

Above: The introduction of radio signalling on the Kyle of Lochalsh line on Friday 7 July saw the beginning of the end for Class 26 locomotives on this famous picturesque route. The radio signalling scheme was inaugurated at a ceremony conducted by BRB Chairman Bob Reid and was to be tested alongside the existing signalling for a six month period to iron out any problems. After this trial eight Inverness-based Class 37 locomotives would be specially nominated to work services on this 63-mile route and would have the cab radio equipment fitted. Illustrating the passing of a long tradition on the Kyle line is this view of Class 26 No 26038 winding towards Kyle at Loch Carron on 27 April with the 0655 from Inverness. *(Peter J Robinson)*

Left: With the Post Office doing a roaring trade judging by the mail bags on the platform, Class 37 No 37114 arrives at Achnasheen with the 1110 Kyle of Lochalsh-Inverness on 18 May. This scene showing the changeover of the token is now but a memory as the time honoured signalling system gave way to the innovative radio signalling on 7 July. *(Colin Keay)*

Track topics

Above: During January 1984 work commenced on the 'dequadrifying' of Ashley Down bank, Bristol. By 28 January the (previously) up main line had been severed prior to slewing above the site of the former Ashley Down station. Powering past the work is Class 50 No 50016 *Barham* with the 0740 Penzance-Liverpool. (*John Chalcraft*)

Right: The date is 12 March and the new Ashley Down alignment is complete. Class 50 No 50008 swings from the Cardiff lines trackbed to the Birmingham line trackbed with ecs for the Sunday Cheltenham - Paddington service. The line in the foreground is the old 'up' Bristol-Cardiff line. All services now use two tracks diverging to the south of Filton Junction station. (*John Chalcraft*)

Right: A scene repeated extensively on BR during 1984 – singling of the line. One such example took place on the Ely-Kings Lynn line on 17 June when the section between Littleport and Downham Market was effected. At Hilgay the level crossing was converted to an AOCR type and this view of the new order is dated 6 October. (*I C Scotchman*)

Left and below: Tracklifting is a sad sight for anyone who is railway-minded and nowadays it is an all too frequent occurrence. The lifting of yards and sidings is inevitable, but when main lines are lifted . . !

Work began in 1984 on lifting the former main line between York (Chaloners Whin Junction) and Selby (Barlby Junction) which was closed when the new Selby Diversion line was commissioned. The down line was lifted first with the demolition trains working from the Selby end towards York and retreating as the track was lifted. The pictures show the first rails lifted at Chaloners Whin and a sleeper recovery train backing down the main line at Riccall on 30 May with Class 20 Nos 20029 and 20093 in charge. *(Murray Brown; D B Stacey)*

Left: A surprise scheme was implemented in the late summer to replace the up line from Kirkconnel to Thornhill on the Glasgow & South Western line. The track was placed out of use in 1983 following derailment of a freight train. Although daily services on this line are not particularly heavy, the line has strategic importance as a diversion route to the West Coast Main Line and reinstatement of the defunct line would aid the situation on diversion days. In this view, the 0725 Glasgow - Carlisle local heads south on the single track before the reinstatement took place. The date is 7 July and the locomotive is Class 27 No 27022. *(Peter J Robinson)*

Above: Liverpool Lime Street station has been undergoing a £10m redevelopment scheme which began in 1983. The project was planned in three stages and on 29 November Princess Anne officially opened stage two, which included the major alterations and refurbishment to the station. A new concourse building is the centre-piece and incorporates a travel centre, booking office, Travellers Fare Casey Jones buffet and bar. Amenities for BR staff are also incorporated, such as the train announcer's office and the trainmens' signing-on point. Another noticeable improvement has been refurbishment and extension of the concourse. The station stonework has been restored and the entrance from Lime Street has been vastly improved. BR is also paying for the £2½m renovation of the Victorian trainshed roof, which is part of the third and final stage of the redevelopment and due for completion in 1985. During excavations in connection with the extension of the concourse, artifacts dating from the Liverpool & Manchester Railway were found, including part of the mechanism used in the pulley system which hauled the first trains up the gradient to Edge Hill. These pictures show the excellent improvements to the frontage of Lime Street station and a view of the extended concourse with the new information display. The photos are dated 20 December. *(Both: Colin Boocock)*

Right: White terrazo tiles, hanging baskets, a hostess kiosk, a micro-dot train indicator (the first to be installed on a Scottish Region station) and no platform barriers all show how much Inverness station has been improved for the 1984 season. This photograph was dated 18 September. *(Tom Noble)*

Below: Stranraer can be a bleak place for passengers transferring between the trains and ferries and 1984 saw the benefits of a £500 000 scheme to improve drastically passenger amenities at this port. Covered walkways extending almost to the ferries' berths have been provided and the station building facade was reclad. The 300 000 passengers which annually use Stranraer station will also have the benefit of modernised waiting room and booking office facilities. 1984 saw the introduction of reduced journey times of about 2½ hours to and from Glasgow as a result of the rostering of Class 47 locomotives. One such train is shown here, the 1100 to Euston on 3 September with No 47597 at its head. One of the new walkways is shown in the picture, although one does wonder if the design is in keeping with the surroundings. *(Colin Boocock)*

Passenger   improvements

Left: A last look at the old booking office at York, taken on 21 February. It is hard to believe that this was a temporary structure, erected after the war damage to the station in April 1942! *(D B Stacey)*

Below: The decrepit station at Bedford St Johns was closed at the start of the summer timetable and replaced by a new £40 000 single platform, 200 yards from the old structure. In addition the service from Bletchley was extended to Bedford Midland by using a ¾-mile former goods line which has been realigned and resignalled at a cost of £110 000. Another improvement has been the introduction of a new service of through trains from Bletchley to Kettering. Saying farewell to the old Bedford St Johns station is a twin Class 104 dmu forming the 1720 to Bletchley on 23 April. *(Rodney Lissenden)*

Below
Left: It is hard to believe that this construction is one of London's main terminal stations but *Jane's Railway Year* kids you not! Beneath the girders and portacabins is a listed facade which belongs to Fenchurch Street station. Work started in 1984 on a £28m development scheme for this former LT&SR commuter station. The facade is being retained under the scheme, which will provide office and shop accommodation. This view of the front of Fenchurch Street was taken on 31 October. *(Rodney Lissenden)*

Right: Only the Class 302s will remain in this picture following the rebuilding of Fenchurch Street station. Sets 302306 and 302225 wait for their next turns on 31 October. *(Rodney Lissenden)*

Depots
opened
& shut

Right: It makes a pleasant change to portray a locomotive maintenance depot being *opened* on BR and so this picture has more than earned its place in this year's *JRY.* Now, what other region has a forward looking philosophy, sets the trends and leads the others from open stations to hostesses? Good old ScotRail is the answer and this depot was opened at Thornton Junction on 11 October. A total of 15 Class 08s are allocated there and one of these, No 08761, is seen outside the new depot on 31 December. *(Tom Noble)*

Centre: Corkerhill depot, Glasgow was officially 'switched on' at a ceremony on 28 September. This depot will maintain the new Class 319 emus being built for the Ayrshire electrification project. This view of Corkerhill was taken on 7 October and shows two Class 303 emus, soon to celebrate their 25th anniversary, and, on the left, the versatile TDB 977177, formerly SC55015, which serves as a Sandite unit, police patrol vehicle and route learning car. *(Tom Noble)*

Below: Northwich depot finally closed in December 1984. it did not have an allocation and was only used for stabling. Most frequent occupants in 1984 were the new providers of power for the Peak Forest limestone trains, Class 20s. On 20 September the depot was playing host to Nos 20185 and 20153 and the preserved LMS coach No 4380 owned by the 8E Association (8E was the former depot code). *(Michael Rhodes)*

BR TRAFFIC

The inauguration of the quarter-hourly Gatwick Express service with refurbished Mk 2 stock and Class 73/1 locomotives on a 30-minute timing from Victoria to Gatwick was one of BR's best achievements in the year. The new service suffered one unfortunate setback, though: the locomotives suffered from severe problems with electrical switchgear being damaged by arcing. Remedial investigations and attention were hurriedly implimented and the service duly returned to normal and attracted more business than BR had budgeted for. The following portfolio shows the new service, its promotion, its setbacks and its success.

'Gatwick Express' in service. Reliveried No 73133 leads a down working past Coulsdon North on 2 September. Headcode 30 signals that this train will travel via Redhill rather than the Quarry Line. On this occasion this was due to Sunday engineering work, although a couple of weekday services were booked to take this route. *(Les Nixon)*

Gatwick take-off

Above: In March, a Gatwick Express 6-coach promotional train toured the country for the benefit of the travel trade and visited Wolverhampton and Chester (12 March), Manchester (13 March), Sheffield, York, Leeds (14 March) and Newcastle (15 March). Class 33/1 No 33113 provided the power, visiting parts other 33s fail to reach. Its appearance in such unlikely places as Sheffield and Newcastle made it one of the most unusual workings of the year. The brake vehicle was a standard Mk 1 as the special GLV vehicles were not completed. Unfortunately, the inclusion of this brake detracted from the visual image of the set. The entourage is pictured at York on 14 March when it was en route to Sheffield. This view recalls memories of the Cliffe-Uddingston cement trains which ran in the 1960s and which brought Class 33s to York and, sometimes, beyond. A Southern Region crew drove the Class 33/1 with conductors provided by the LMR and ER. *(David Stacey)*

Centre: Prior to the introduction of the new service, crew training runs took place on several routes, one of which was down the ex-LBSC main line to Brighton. Brake testing also took place between Woking and Basingstoke. In this picture No 73109 approaches Preston Park with a 1455 London Bridge-Brighton crew training run on 31 March. *(Alex Dasi-Sutton)*

Left: The GLV vehicles were converted at Eastleigh from Class 414 (2HAP) motor coaches and a total of ten were provided for the new service. Of the passenger carrying vehicles, 67 second class and 10 first class vehicles were nominated and refurbished at Derby Litchurch Lane Works. The total package of GLV, TFO and seven TSOs was designated Class 488 and nine sets are formed from these vehicles, with the remaining four second class, one first class and one GLV as spare. GLV No 9101 leads a crew-training trip at Brighton on 24 February. *(Alex Dasi-Sutton)*

Left and centre: The best laid plans ... By the time a third Class 73/1 had suffered fire damage as a result of arcing current, the matter was considered so serious that the Gatwick Express service was withdrawn on Sunday 5 August after drivers expressed their concern over personal safety. The fires had occurred on Nos 73104, 73129 and 73142 and had all taken place after the train had reached the down main at Battersea Park. An emergency replacement service was implemented using 4CIG and 4VEP units and on 8 August, four out of the seven diagrams reverted to locomotive-haulage using 6-coach sets and double-headed Class 73/1s on diesel power only. These two pictures illustrate the temporary arrangements instigated to cater for the problem. Nos 73138 and 73140 approach Gatwick with the 1300 from Victoria on 9 August whilst on 13 August, Class 411 4CEP No 7153 leads a substitute emu Gatwick Express train into Gatwick. *(Alex Dasi-Sutton; Colin Boocock)*

Below: To determine the cause of the arcing at Battersea Park, instrumented tests were conducted on the evenings of 6 and 7 August using No 73123 *Gatwick Express* and a set of vehicles. The proceedings were also videoed. Spark guards were subsequently fitted to selected Class 73/1s and these can be seen in this view of No 73133 at Salfords in charge of the 1300 Victoria-Gatwick on 30 August. The same day GLV No 9104 leads the 1705 Gatwick-Victoria at Merstham with Class 73/1 No 73123 on the rear. *(Both: Colin J Marsden)*

BR hit by pit strike

Above: Knottingley depot in the heart of the Yorkshire coalfield. The picture tells the story as several million pounds worth of machinery stand idle. This depressing sight was taken early on in the dispute on 17 April, when 13 Class 56 locomotives were deprived of work. Nearest the camera are Nos 56106, 56022 and 56003. What was so sad was that railwaymen helped to wreck their own industry by supporting the miners. This took the form of not moving iron ore from Immingham to Scunthorpe and Port Talbot to Llanwern, as well as not moving coal from those pits which continued or returned to production. *(Gavin Morrison)*

Left: Some coal traffic did run during the dispute, though, especially from the Nottinghamshire field, and it was noticeable that there was a preference to use the new Class 58 locomotives on the residual traffic in preference to Class 56. Emerging from Alfreton tunnel is a southbound mgr on 2 May behind Class 58 No 58001. The dispute had repercussions on many other traffics, one notable example being the lucrative fly ash traffic, much of which is routed to Fletton, Peterborough. This loss also contributed dramatically to the severe downturn in revenue which would have such an adverse bearing on the 1984 accounts, with the strike costing BR around £5m per week. *(Brian Cuttell)*

Left: The miners' dispute resulted in the running of more oil trains to those power stations in the Trent Valley that are oil-fired as well as coal-burning. Class 47/3 No 47304 waits at Nuneaton Trent Valley station on 23 May with a special empty tank train returning to Thames Haven refinery from Rugeley. *(Paul A Biggs)*

WR timetable changes

Top: An innovation on the Western Region for the summer timetable was the introduction of heavy locomotive-hauled services which were given the now customary silly title, this time 'Jumbo' trains. The WR's intention was to effect an improvement in the operating cost per mile/seat but, of course, this was at the expense of increased journey times compared with HST. Two Paddington-Penzance and one Paddington-Paignton trains were duly rostered for Class 50s and 13/14/15-coach formations. This move released some HSTs for use on other workings, notably the new roster to Malvern (see p 108) and the return to some Oxford shuttle services in an effort to combat coach competition. On 7 July Class 50 No 50009 *Conqueror* powers the 1340 Paddington-Penzance loaded to 15 bogies past Aller Junction. *(Steve Turner)*

Left: Also in May 1984 the WR re-introduced the title 'Torbay Express', now used for the locomotive-hauled 1035 Paddington-Paignton service and the 1105 return. Thus the pomp and ceremony which accompanied the introduction of a HST on this service in 1983 was short-lived! A headboard was provided for both services but was only used for the first two weeks. On 18 May the down train arrives at Westbury behind Class 50 No 50030 *Repulse*. The revised track layout is evident in this picture, brought into use with the new power box four days previously. The former up main line (behind the first coach) is now a siding. *(G F Gillham)*

Below: With the introduction of the 1984 timetable, the 0920 Bristol-Paddington was diverted to run via Trowbridge, the Westbury North curve and the Berks and Hants line, this being the first daily use of the Westbury North curve except for engineering diversions. On 6 September the train was formed of all first class stock, mainly Mk 1, and is seen here approaching Hawkeridge Junction, Westbury behind Class 50 No 50050 *Fearless*. *(G F Gillham)*

WCML changes

Right: Highlight of the LMR's new timetable on 14 May was the introduction of accelerated services between Glasgow and Euston, made possible by 110 mph running with Class 87 locomotives fitted with the Brecknell-Willis pantograph. Four services in each direction were authorised to travel at this speed, these being the 0945, 1145, 1650 and 1730 from Euston and the 0910, 1310, 1510 and the 1710 from Glasgow. In this view the 1650 from Euston hurries past Spring Branch depot, Wigan on 21 June behind reliveried Class 87 No 87012 *Coeur-de-Lion.* Last but one vehicle in the formation is the first of the Mk 3 FOs to be outshopped in the executive livery to match the locomotive. The InterCity Director had hoped to have a complete set in this livery but this was not to be. Also of interest and new in 1984 is the sight of Class 20s on Springs Branch depot. These made their appearance for crew training. *(Tom Heavyside)*

Centre: 1984 will be remembered as the year of the Liverpool Garden Festival. This major tourist attraction brought much business to BR and to capitalise on the publicity the 0900 Euston-Liverpool service was named the 'Festival Rose'. A dirty Class 87 was provided for the inaugural train on 9 May, but at least it was No 87008 *City of Liverpool.* The express is pictured arriving at Lime Street. May we hope that the future will see an end to the pantomime of using stick-on headboards? The case has surely been proven that there is justification for brackets to enable quality headboards to be attached. *(Fred Kerr)*

Below: Class 86/2 No 86231 received its name *Starlight Express* at a ceremony at Euston on 1 October attended by some of the cast from the musical of the same name. Here is a first glimpse of a complete consist of Executive-liveried stock in the shape of a 'Manchester Pullman' set headed by No 86231 passing Milton Keynes on a special working on Saturday 6 October. The Euston-Glasgow 'Nightrider' was renamed 'Starlight Express' as from the date of the naming and the train included a video service. *(Paul D Shannon)*

East Coast loco-hauled

Left: Daytime locomotive-hauled trains on the East Coast Main Line are now a rarity and on 12 May another example made its last run, the 0840 York-Aberdeen and the 1630 return. Here the final 1S12 heads past Heaton on its way north behind Class 47/4 No 47422. *(Neville E Stead)*

Right: However, keeping the spark of locomotive-haulage alive, at least during daytime hours, was a new service during the summer months, the 1305 (Sun) Kings Cross-Dundee. There was no corresponding up working. Reviving memories is this view of the new train leaving Berwick on 22 July with Class 47/4 No 47416 in charge. *(Peter J Robinson)*

Below: On 22 August another 1984 timetable innovation, the 1059 summer weekdays only Kings Cross-Dundee, had very unusual power in the form of Class 27 No 27001. Heading back home, the 27 takes its train past Penmanshiel. Somewhat surprisingly there are no booked workings for Class 26 or 27 south from Edinburgh and those which do appear are deputising for failed Class 47s. *(Peter J Robinson)*

S & C demand confounds BR

The sad and disgraceful saga of the Settle & Carlisle closure proposal plummeted to an abysmal new low with the revelation that the official closure notices had to be issued for a third time because previous notices had not included reference to the fact that a three-mile section of the line fell within the boundary of the Newcastle Transport Users Consultative Committee.

Meanwhile, business boomed during the year, particularly during the spring, as a result of which BR was prompted to cater for the demand firstly by strengthening the normal service train and, secondly, by instituting a relief. But did they advertise it? York station inquiry office did not know of the relief train a day before it commenced! The Settle & Carlisle Joint Action Committee publicised the summer trains from its own resources. This organisation also became a limited company during 1984 to strengthen its position and to combat the BR closure proposal from a more positive advantage point in view of BR's appointment (see *JRY* 1983) of a manager whose remit is to close the line. Reflecting the changing scene on the S&C in 1984 are these pictures.

Above: The first of the summer-only York-Carlisle extras introduced to the S&C returns south on Saturday 14 July with its Mk 1 and Mk 2 mixture, passing Ribblehead Quarry. The decision to run on Sundays involved opening the S&C for scheduled through traffic on this day for the first time for several years. *(David Wilcock)*

Left: To quote a well known American tennis player, "You've got to be kidding", but the station nameboard and the dmu blind does not lie. This was BR's answer to the huge demand for seats on the Settle & Carlisle line in 1984. On Mondays to Fridays a dmu ran as an extra leaving York at 0859 and calling at intermediate major stations to Carlisle, returning at 1500. Does one laugh or cry? Fortunately, common sense prevailed on Saturdays and Sundays when a locomotive-hauled set was provided. This is Carlisle in the rain on 6 August as the York-bound dmu waits for departure. *(R L Patrick)*

Above: Such was the demand for travel in the spring that the morning Leeds-Carlisle service, the 0900 which this year started back at Hull departing at 0738, was steadily strengthened, so much so, that by the time that this picture was taken on 31 March, it was loaded to eleven bogies. Class 45/1 No 45109 crosses Arten Gill viaduct. *(Gavin Morrison)*

And there's not a steam locomotive in sight! These are just ordinary folk wishing to ride the Settle & Carlisle, illustrating the problem which confronted BR when the usual service trains could not cope with the demand, thus necessitating extra vehicles, and ultimately, the provision of an additional train throughout the week. In this picture, Class 45/1 No 45137 arrives at Settle with the 0738 Hull-Carlisle (0900 ex-Leeds) on 7 April. *(Tom Heavyside)*

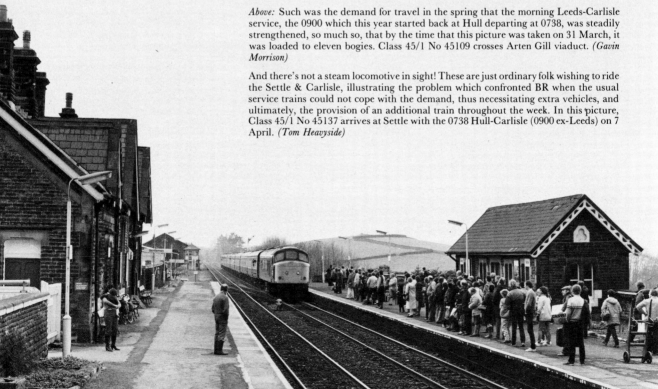

New freight flows

Above: A new service on the West Highland line commenced in January conveying alumina from Blyth to Fort William. The train, 6S56 0712 Blyth-Mallaig Junction Yard utilises BRT (PAF) wagons and Procor vehicles. Both types are illustrated in this view of No 37147 at Possil in north-east Glasgow on 21 August. From September this train was frequently double-headed. The balancing working was 6E46 1519 ex Mallaig Junction Yard. *(Tom Noble)*

Left: A new traffic flow commenced in the summer of 1984 conveying scrap from Barrow to Tinsley. The train, usually entrusted to Class 40 haulage, took the Hellifield road at Carnforth and proceeded to Leeds and thence Sheffield. The scrap train ran twice a week on Tuesdays and Fridays and utilised 15-ton mineral wagons (MSVs). This picture shows the train passing Bentham on the Carnforth to Hellifield line on 19 October. Heading the train is the last vacuum-braked Class 40 No 40009, which had two weeks service left, being withdrawn on 5 November due to rough riding. *(David Wilcock)*

Above: Speedlink continued its success in 1984 with the introduction of further services and Railfreight celebrated the inauguration of its 150th Speedlink service at a ceremony at Willesden on 1 October when a new working to Mossend commenced on a daily basis. Illustrating 1984's expansion and also the forays which took the Class 58s to Manchester for the first time is this view of 7M60 1246 Ashburys-Toton. This train frequently consisted of only one vehicle as depicted in this view of No 58003 at Chinley East Junction on 30 August. *(Steve Turner)*

Left: Although the end is in sight for the faithful mineral wagon (MSV) it was still in extensive use in 1984, usually utilised in the conveyance of scrap. However, one long-distance haul inaugurated during the year was 7A12 1410 Peak Forest South-Bletchley conveying limestone. Class 47/3 No 47322 was officiating on this duty when pictured at Peak Forest on 6 November. *(John Tuffs)*

Peak destroyed in nuclear safety test

Left and below: On 17 July took place one of the most bizarre spectacles seen on the British railway scene for many years – the deliberate wrecking of a locomotive and train. This was an attempt to show that rail is the safest form of transport by which to move nuclear flasks containing irradiated fuel. The simulated crash involved a Class 46 Locomotive, No 46009, and three Mk 1 coaches being run at 100 mph into an upturned nuclear flask wagon. The scene of this sad display was BR's test track at Old Dalby, Leicestershire. The cost? A staggering £1.5m, and that was not all. The Central Electricity Generating Board are spending a total of no less than £4m to convince the public that nuclear power is a safe commodity. The CEGB paid BR £16 750 for No 46009, considerably more than its scrap price, and £2100 for the three Mk 1 vehicles, which was the correct figure on the open market. The exercise was carefully timed so as to coincide with the national television news, which screened the incident live, but the smash was delayed for a few minutes whilst protesters were removed from the vicinity. The two official photographs depict the positioning of the 48-tonne flask wagon and the impact zone of the locomotive. *(Both: CEGB)*

Below: Besides No 46009, No 46023 was also secured for this exercise as a standby. Both locomotives had been withdrawn from BR service specially for this test and had been given the Departmental numbers of 97401 and 97402, although neither carried the new numbers. It was imperative for the locomotive to reach 100 mph and as the maximum speed was 90 mph for a Class 46, Toton depot modified the locomotives to meet the requirement. However, during tests, No 46023 could only reach 97 mph and so it fell to No 46009 to be wrecked. These pictures taken the day before at Old Dalby show the standby loco on the left with No 46009 being prepared with instruments to measure and record the devastation. *(Both: D J Howdle)*

Above: The moment of impact – broadcast live for the entertainment of millions – as No 46009 ploughs into the flask-carrying vehicle on 17 July. *(CEGB)*

Centre and below: The three coaches used in the actual crash were SK E25154, TSO M4514 and SK E25564 (very naughty running a train without a brake vehicle!). While No 46009 was hurtling to destruction, No 46023 and another three vehicles, SK E25447, CK E7970 and SK E25038 were standing at Edwalton, eight miles further north at the extremity of the test track in the event of No 46009 failing. The actual crash was watched by thousands of spectators, many having arrived by special train from London. The Magnox Mark M2c flask emerged unscathed. No 46009 did not. The driver's control handle was the object which travelled furthest from the crash location. Scrap processor Vic Berry of Leicester later received the contract to cut up the remains of the locomotive and coaches. And did it prove that transporting flasks by rail was safe? Greenpeace, the environmentalists, did not think so, claiming that the test was not conducted in a way to demonstrate effectively the object of the exercise. While the arrangements made by the CEGB were exemplary, there were many people who did not need convincing by such an exercise and who would have preferred the money – their money – spent more profitably in keeping electricity prices stable for a longer period. *(Both: D J Howdle)*.

New HST destinations

Release of HSTs from some West of England services made available one set to work a new service through to Great Malvern. It left Paddington at 1025 and returned at 1343. The Cotswold route has seen a remarkable revival in recent years following the run-down of services and the severe pruning of locomotive-hauled trains on this line. One important bonus with HST operation was that passengers on this route had access to a full buffet service. The up train is shown with these views of the 1343 from Great Malvern heading out of Moreton-in-Marsh on 27 October with power car No 43036 leading and the same train approaching Finstock on 11 July with Nos 43010 and 43029 providing the horsepower. *(Paul D Shannon; Paul A Biggs)*

Top: Inverness was placed on the HST map as from the summer timetable with a daily service to and from Kings Cross, the first through working between the Highland and English capitals. The departures were the 0720 from Inverness, arriving at 1600 and the 1200 off Kings Cross arriving at 2050. These trains were given the title 'The Highland Chieftain' and, in addition, HST power car No 43092 received this name at a ceremony at Inverness on 15 May. Because of this naming Class 87 No 87023 lost its *Highland Chieftain* name and ran for the rest of the year nameless. This rather dubious practice of denaming locomotives never meets with approval from the railway fraternity and one wonders if BR derives any benefit from such moves. Presenting a new sight at Inverness is the 0720 HST to London pictured on 26 May. *(Fred Kerr)*

Centre: This is *Highland Chieftain* (43092) on 'The Highland Chieftain' and it was not fixed for *Jane's Railway Year*! The date was 22 September and the location is Aviemore. These HST services were originally listed as ending on 29 September but they were continued into the winter timetable. *(Tom Noble)*

Bottom: An innovation in 1984 was InterCity Director Cyril Bleasdale's decision to route HSTs from the South West under the 25kV wires. Thus both Manchester Piccadilly and Liverpool Lime Street were to be seen hosting HSTs as from 14 May. This previously unfamiliar sight is illustrated at Manchester Piccadilly, by the 1039 to Paignton with power car No 43189 leading on 7 July. *(Tom Heavyside)*

Below: Liverpool was serviced by one HST working daily, the 0743 from Bristol and the 1210 departure to Plymouth. This latter train prepares to leave Lime Street on 4 August. *(Tom Heavyside)*

Service diverted . . .

Above: The major innovation for NE-SW services in 1984 was the re-routing of traffic via Doncaster and the Selby Diversion instead of the Swinton & Knottingley route from York to Sheffield, leaving the S&K the preserve of mgr trains. Memories of more important times are provided with this view of the 0745 Plymouth-Newcastle heading past Ferrybridge on 17 March. *(Peter M Marsh)*

Right: By traversing the Selby diversion and thence the Doncaster to Sheffield line via Mexborough, HSTs were given in the order of 51 minutes for the York to Sheffield section, including a stop at Doncaster. This compares to 58 or 60 minutes for the direct route with its many mining subsidence track restrictions. Here 1E30, the 0700 Plymouth-Newcastle service, approaches Mexborough on 28 July with power cars Nos 43148/43147 officiating. *(John Tuffs)*

Above: Another change of route took place with the start of the summer timetable when the 'Bradford Executive' began calling at Leeds, hitherto having avoided the city by means of the Wortley curve. Pictured on what is now a rare stretch for haulage fans – the Wortley curve linking Wortley South with Wortley West Junctions – is the last 0736 Bradford-Kings Cross headed by power car No 43194 on Friday 11 May. *(John Fozard)*

. . . and withdrawn

Below: Despite its 330 000 population, Hull was deprived of its mid-day HST services to and from London as from 14 May. The 1140 and 1540 from Hull were abolished and the 0804 and 1204 from Kings Cross ceased to run through to Hull, terminating instead at Doncaster. It was "all change" at Doncaster for the good people of Hull with the exception of one HST in each direction, 'The Hull Executive' at 0700 off Hull and 1730 return off Kings Cross. Gilberdyke is the setting for this picture showing the 'good old days' before 14 May. The 1140 service from Hull heads towards London on 28 April. *(Peter M Marsh)*

Above: Major changes took place on the East Suffolk line in 1984 with the passing of an era on the cessation of locomotive-hauled workings to and from London, Liverpool Street. This line in the 1950s even boasted a named train, 'The Easterling', but from 14 May passengers on the line could expect no better than a dmu service. On the last day of locomotive working, Saturday 12 May, the final trains are illustrated. Class 37 No 37049 'The East Suffolk Line Broadsman' carrying a farewell headboard draws the last 0717 Lowestoft-Liverpool Street out of Saxmundham.

East Suffolk service cutback

Centre: The last down working, the 1700 from Liverpool Street, was in the hands of No 37115, which is seen taking the East Suffolk line at Ipswich. (both: *John A Day*)

Right: The new and unwelcome order on the East Suffolk line: dmus. This is the first dmu from Lowestoft on the first day of the summer timetable, 14 May, consisting of two 3-car Met-Camm sets forming the 0715 from the East Coast resort. It is seen at Wickham Market. BR maintained that the locomotive-hauled services were poorly patronised and thus did not justify their retention. In addition, the fitting of radio receivers in connection with the radio signalling being installed on the ESL would be an undesirable restriction on locomotives which would have to remain in the vicinity of Ipswich. This argument was refuted by those with a knowledge of the radio signalling which BR intend to operate, as portable receivers are available which could be fitted to any locomotive and not just to a dedicated fleet. (*Ian Cowley*)

Departures & Main line Arrivals

From	To	Plat	Arr	Dep	Mins late
STARTING TODAY NEW DIRECT SERVICES WILL OPERATE BETWEEN LEEDS AND PRESTON-BLACKPOOL. PLEASE ENQUIRE FOR FULL DETAILS...					
	MORECAMBE	6B		0835	
MANCHESTER	YORK	9C	0830	0837	
SCARBORO	BRADFORD	12	0837	0840	
VIA HGATE	POPPLETON	1B		0842	
HARROGATE	LONDON-KX	5	0835	0845	
	SOUTHPORT	10B		0850	
VIA BFORD	BLACKPOOL	3A		0853	
	CASTLEFORD	12		0900	
VIA HGATE	KNARESBORO	1B		0900	

Copy pit revival

Left: A new service was inaugurated on 1 October between Leeds and Preston via the previously freight-only Copy Pit line. Six trains were provided in each direction on Mondays to Saturdays (five on Saturdays) and one train in each direction ran through to and from Blackpool. Sadly it was a dmu service with the full journey taking just under two hours, which is fine if you are a dmu fan! Revealing all at Leeds on the first day is the information monitor. *(Tony Woof)*

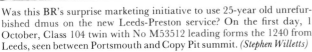

Was this BR's surprise marketing initiative to use 25-year old unrefurbished dmus on the new Leeds-Preston service? On the first day, 1 October, Class 104 twin with No M53512 leading forms the 1240 from Leeds, seen between Portsmouth and Copy Pit summit. *(Stephen Willetts)*

Below: However, the hand that gives also takes away and 1984 was to be the last year that the Sheffield-Blackpool summer dated trains ran via the L&Y Calder Valley line and the Copy Pit route. This was a popular train for Class 37 haulage fans and offered a rare chance to travel behind loco-hauled stock over the predominantly freight Copy Pit line. Class 37 No 37031 was rostered to work the last train of the season, 1M89 0749 Sheffield-Blackpool and the 1E45 1240 return on September 1 and the latter train is seen at Nott Wood viaduct, Lydgate, descending to the Calder Valley main line. *(Stephen Willetts)*

Although it was known that BR was intending to inaugurate a passenger service over the Copy Pit line from Preston to Leeds, the National & Provincial Building Society sponsored a new service from Burnley to Bradford for the benefit of its employees in moving between the head offices of the Burnley Building Society and the Provincial Building Society at Bradford. These two merged in 1983. The train commenced running on 14 May and the public could also use it. It left Preston at 0715 and returned from Bradford at 1625 (Mon-Wed) and 1734 (Thurs-Fri). On the first day the evening train is pictured near Portsmouth sporting a stick-on headboard proclaiming 'National & Provincial'. *(Richard Fox)*

Cross-country

Above: BR in 1984 continued to develop the market for people who want to travel to other places than the capital, with a further effort to offer the public through trains to destinations which hitherto required a change of train. One example in the 1984 timetable was the 1320 Glasgow-Cardiff service and the 0810 from Cardiff in the return direction. Nearing journey's end on 24 May is the 1320 from Glasgow seen here passing Severn Tunnel Junction behind Class 50 No 50048 *Dauntless. (Michael Rhodes)*

Below: One wonders what Hull residents thought of their new timetable on 14 May for with the exception of the 0700 and 0800 trains they lost their HST services to Kings Cross and, instead, gained a new London train – to Paddington! – well not quite, it actually went to Brighton but the balancing working came from Paddington. Confused? So were Hull residents. The story started at Paddington at 0650 when off set a new service to Hull arriving at 1245, having collected many Hull-bound people at Reading, Birmingham, Derby, Sheffield and Doncaster. Sadly, it was asking too much for a simple return journey for at 1322 the set departed for Sheffield, where it joined with the 1400 from Leeds and continued via its outward route until Reading was reached, from where the train proceeded to Brighton via Kensington Olympia and East Croydon. It could only happen in England! Just to prove that it worked, here is the inaugural 0650 passing Gilberdyke on time on 14 May. Class 47/4 No 47437 is in charge. *(Michael Rhodes)*

Above: Scotland to Poole? HST or Class 87 to Kings Cross or Euston respectively followed by a sprightly run from Waterloo in a 4REP+4TC. There was an alternative in 1984 with the start of a new service from Edinburgh and Glasgow through to Poole via Birmingham, Reading and Basingstoke. It did take just a bit longer! Southbound the train left Edinburgh at 0940 and Glasgow at 0950, combining at Carstairs and arrived at Poole at 1915. Heading north, it was a 0734 departure from Poole and an arrival time of 1637 at Glasgow and 1640 at Edinburgh. Powering through the Lune Valley is the northbound train on 9 June in the capable hands of Class 87 No 87013 *John O' Gaunt.* (*Peter J Robinson*)

Right: To provide West Midlands passengers with a connection into a mid-morning Sealink Harwich-Hook of Holland sailing, from the start of the May 1984 timetable a Parkeston Quay service previously starting at Peterborough was extended back to Wolverhampton. The 0530 starting time calls for a strong constitution but does avoid the luggage-laden transit across the capital. Leading the way with this service near Soham on 16 June is No 31277. (*John C Baker*)

Accident report

1984 was a bad year for BR in terms of major mishaps. 18 people were killed and many more were seriously injured. While several of the accidents gave little indication of their cause, those which did revealed that, as expected, there was no common link and initial evidence showed that amongst the causes for some of the accidents were fractured equipment, stray animals, poorly maintained track and, sadly, the possibility of a driver being under the influence of drink.

Below and top right: Some £2m worth of damage was caused on 11 October at Wembley when the 1754 Euston-Bletchley, formed of Class 310 units Nos 067 and 086, collided with a Freightliner which had been given the road north out of Willesden FLT yard. Sadly, three people died and 18 were injured out of the 500 on board the emu. A file on the case was later sent to the Director of Public Prosecutions, an action which caused some adverse comment from the Inspecting Officer. He was denied the chance to interview the driver as the circumstances of the accident were sub judice and thus the Inspecting Officer was denied his duty by law to ascertain the cause of the crash. The photos were taken on the following morning, 12 October, by which time the leading two vehicles had been righted and moved into Wembley station platform. *(Both: Mick Roberts)*

Centre right: This picture shows the remains of Class 45/1 No 45147 after it ran into the rear of the 0900 Stanlow-Leeds oil train at Weaste, Salford, on 4 December when hauling the 1005 Liverpool-Scarborough train. The driver was killed, as was a 70-year old passenger. Fire engulfed the locomotive, the first coach was gutted and the second badly burnt. The oil train was moving at the time, having just started to accelerate from a signal stop. Initial indications pointed to the express overrunning a red signal. *(A Sherratt)*

Left: On 24 June the 2050 Aberdeen-Kings Cross sleeper crashed at Morpeth after taking the severe curve at excess speed. The astonishing revelation came to light that following the crash at the same point in 1969 when a north-bound Deltic-hauled sleeper had taken the curve at 80 mph, the AWS warning magnets which the Inspecting Officer has recommended to be fitted when the line speed was suddenly reduced, had only been fitted on the down line as the up line had a gradual speed reduction limit leading to Morpeth and thus did not qualify! Penny-pinching to the extreme! The driver of Class 47/4 No 47452 was subsequently charged with being under the influence of alcohol. Miraculously, only two people were hurt and this was stated to be a reflection on the construction of the Mk 3 sleeper coach. Two houses were damaged by the derailed vehicles and whilst the smash was being cleared, Anglo-Scottish traffic used the Blyth & Tyne route which joins the ECML just north of Morpeth station. *(Malcolm G Charlton)*

Below left and below: Luckily there were not fatalities on 1 August when the 0730 Leeds-Edinburgh HST toppled down an embankment at Birtley, Tyne Yard. The HST had been routed round the back of Tyne Yard to give staff safe clearance in attending to a failed locomotive on the up fast. Travelling at 40 mph, the HST derailed, sending three coaches off the rails and two down an embankment. Twenty people needed treatment for minor injuries. A track chargeman subsequently admitted at the inquiry conducted by the Inspecting Officer Major Peter Olver that he had rushed an inspection of the track because it had been raining and had thus failed to see the two broken bolts which were the cause of the crash. The Inspecting Officer was also concerned with the way track irregularities were administered in the area concerned and, in particular, following up reported defects. The pictures show the broken bolts responsible and the aftermath. *(Malcolm G Charlton; Peter J Robinson)*

Centre left: Oops! Class 87 No 87023 ran into the rear of an electrification maintenance train at Rugby whilst hauling the 1200 Wolverhampton-Euston on 9 December. This locomotive was to have received the name *Royal Mail Midlands* early in 1985 in connection with the issue of a set of railway stamps but, instead, Class 86/2 No 86226 *Mail* was substituted. Here is the nameless Class 87 being cut free on the same evening. The rear vehicle of the overhead line train was ADM 395401, a 1924-built LMS period 1 TK No M1260M which was converted to its electrification role in 1958; repeat was! *(J Critchley)*

Centre right: The buckled remains of a 100-ton tanker wagon awaits demolition in the middle of Summit tunnel. The 6M08 0140 Haverton Hill-Glazebrook formed of 13 tanks derailed ¾-mile inside the 2885-yard tunnel between Todmorden and Rochdale in the early hours of 20 December. The fourth and fifth wagons left the track and caught fire but the locomotive and first three wagons were unscathed. Such was the inferno that temperatures in the tunnel reached 1200°C, local residents were evacuated and the A6033 main Todmorden to Rochdale road which crosses over the tunnel was closed. The fire raged for several days but the 140-year old tunnel built by George Stephenson had been constructed to such a quality that damage to the lining was considered repairable, although the tunnel would be out of commission for at least three months. A broken axle was found in the tunnel some way from the scene of the accident to give investigators a positive indication of what caused one of the most spectacular mishaps in rail history.

Knotty
specials

Opposite
Top: The North Staffordshire Railway gained much publicity and goodwill in 1984 with a series of dmu charter trains through the delightful Churnet Valley. Pictured at Cheddleton on 25 February is the 3-car Class 104 inaugural NSR-sponsored special from Crewe to Oakamoor. Regular runs began on 22 April. *(Bill Chapman)*

Bottom: The 'Churnetrail' specials ran Sundays and Bank Holidays from 22 April until October. Here the first of the regular specials is being flagged away by Mr Alan Jackson, Chairman, Cheddleton Parish Council. On his left is Mr Philip Oldfield, Chairman, North Staffordshire Railway, whose base is at Cheddleton. *(Staffordshire Sentinel Newspapers)*

'Midlands Link' inaugurated

Right: A new service commenced on 14 May running between Birmingham and Nottingham on a two-hour frequency. Three days earlier, civic dignatories were taken for a ride along the route in Tyseley's black windowed 3-car Met-Camm unit Nos M53307/59107/53323. Sporting the service's new title, the Class 101 set stands at Nottingham after arrival. *(Steve Knight)*

Below: The new 'Midland Link' service from Birmingham to Nottingham was normally worked by Class 120 sets. Seen departing from Burton-on-Trent is the 0733 Lincoln St Marks-Birmingham service on the first day of the timetable, 14 May, formed by a 120 comprising vehicles M53742 + M59268 + M53654. *(John Tuffs)*

Oban specials

Above: Following the pattern set in 1983, the Sundays only Edinburgh-Oban excursions operated from 1 July to 9 September, again using a 'push-pull' set plus a buffet with an Ethel providing power for the air-conditioning and public address. One variation for 1984 was that the Class 37 and Ethel took over from a Class 47 at Cowlairs, instead of powering the train from Edinburgh. In this picture, No 37264 and Ethel 2 are seen backing onto the train at Cowlairs signalbox on 26 August. At the other end can be seen No 47555 *The Commonwealth Spirit*, which brought the train from Edinburgh. *(Tom Noble)*

Below: A Sunday Oban-Glasgow and return service was introduced in 1984, operating from July 1-Sept 9. It utilised one locomotive and stock stabled over the weekend at Oban and left Oban at 12.25, returning from Glasgow Queen St at 17.20. An Oban crew worked both trains throughout. From a pictorial point of view, the Sunday train was indistinguishable from the normal weekday services. However, this is 37051 and the 12.25 from Oban on Sunday August 26, passing Westerton station.

"The freight train now arrived at platform 1 is the 1345 from Aberdeen". This picture shows passengers alighting from BR's first timetabled mixed freight/passenger, air/vacuum-braked train at Inverness, a service enterprisingly inaugurated on 26 March to capture freight traffic to and from the Far North. Class 47 No 47118 had powered the train from Inverness on the date of this picture, 17 July. *(Colin Boocock)*

Mixed train stages come back

The specially adapted Freightliner wagon is sent forward to Wick on the 1735 from Inverness to Wick and Thurso. This strange arrangement is depicted here with No 37114 heading this train out of Muir of Ord on 22 September. *(Steve Turner)*

Container wagons worked in passenger trains from Aberdeen are loaded and unloaded at Wick by this road crane. One of the Freightliner vehicles can be seen on the left. This photograph is dated 4 July. *(Tom Noble)*

The long way round

Above: Long-distance Sunday rail travellers often don't know what they are letting themselves in for: engineering work frequently calls for major diversions from established routes which may well please the fans but frequently frustrate and confuse the innocent customer.

For five successive Sundays early in 1984 Waterloo-Exeter services were routed via Southampton to allow pw engineers to work between Andover and Salisbury. On the initial Sunday, 19 January, No 50032 *Courageous* hurries through Dean, between Salisbury and Romsey, with the 0945 Exeter St Davids-Waterloo. *(G F Gillham)*

Below: Appreciative clients on the 1105 Plymouth-Manchester enjoy rare mileage as their train approaches Sea Mills, on the Avonmouth Loop, again behind No 50032 *Courageous*. Complete severance of the normal route between Dr Days Junction and Filton Junction (see p90) necessitated this unusual diversion. *(John Chalcraft)*

Above: Sunday engineering work near Bristol Parkway from 29 January to 13 May led to lengthy diversions for several North East/South West services, including the 1945 Aberdeen-Bristol sleeper, which travelled from Birmingham via Oxford, Didcot and Bath. Leaving the western exit from Box Tunnel with this train on 29 April is No 45150. *(G F Gillham)*

Below: The retention of the Settle & Carlisle for diversionary purposes has long been one of the main reasons for objectors to the closure proposal but 13 May saw the last Sunday diversions. Previous timetables have hitherto shown scheduled diversions via this route but the 1984 winter timetable did not do so. As a result BR's pantomime degenerated into pure farce for, being denied the S&C, the Sunday 0935 Liverpool-Glasgow was timetabled via, would you believe, York? This train finally arrived in Glasgow Central at 1720. This is the ultimate example of a 'roundabout' train! Recalling the days when common sense did prevail is this view of the 0925 Carlisle-Euston crossing Arten Gill viaduct on 13 May behind Class 47/4 No 47413. *(D B Stacey)*

Trans-Pennine super-tanker

In May began running one of the heaviest trains to run in Britain and certainly the heaviest to run over the Pennines. It was known as the hot oil train and ran as 6E49 from Stanlow to Teesport. Frequently loaded to 18 100-tonne tankers, the train was rostered for two Class 56 locomotives as far as Healey Mills, where two Class 37s continued with the train to Teeside. These two pictures show this impressive train in action.

Above: On 8 June the hot oil train had 17 tankers and Nos 56108 and 56098 work flat out up Miles Platting Bank with rear end assistance provided by Class 25 No 25095. *(Gavin Morrison)*

Below: One evening in June Nos 56129 and 56132 with 18 on pass Stanlow station and sidings shortly after leaving Shell's refinery. *(David Hunt)*

'Northern Belle' revival

Left: The 'Northern Belle' returned to the rails after an absence of 50 years when the new train carrying this title began running from Aberdeen to Dufftown. The service, which utilised the vehicles off the previous night's 'Nightrider' from London, was a joint venture run by Grampian Railtours with the co-operation of BR, Aberdeen Tourist Board and Glenfiddich Distillery. Lunch, afternoon tea and a visit to the distillery coupled with a 128-mile journey cost only £15 per person. The first train departed on 6 June with Class 47/4 No 47429 in charge and is seen near Loch Park near Dufftown. *(D M May)*

Centre: The delightful rural nature of the Dufftown branch can be glimpsed from this picture showing No 47485 winding along the valley bottom after leaving Dufftown on 25 August. *(Les Nixon)*

Bottom: The 'Northern Belle' ran twice weekly on Wednesdays and Saturdays between 6 June and 29 August. Such was the popularity, however, that extra runs were made, including private charter trips. On 26 August the Michelin company ran a private charter which involved two trains. Here No 47428 sets back with its train at Dufftown in readiness to leave at 1700 while the second train behind No 47409 would leave at 1740. *(D M May)*

Van innovations

Above: A new parcels service commenced on 24 January from Stoke-on-Trent to Peterborough. The photograph shows Class 31 No 31295 passing Sutton Bonnington near Kegworth hauling three vans on this service, the 3E25 0912 from Stoke, on its second day, 25 January. *(John Tuffs)*

Below: Electro-diesel No 73101 *Brighton Evening Argus* passes Shortlands on 23 June with a special London Victoria-Dover Western Docks van train run to convey baggage for Cosmos tour participants who were journeying by a preceding emu. This working occurred on a regular basis during the summer months. *(Rodney Lissenden)*

LRT AND METROS

Significant developments took place on both the country's main non-BR 'suburban railway' systems, London Regional Transport and the Tyneside Metro, but soon there may be more concerns on which to report for the success of the Metro on Tyneside has spurred other Passenger Transport Executives to consider the benefits of similar systems within their areas. In 1984 the West Midlands PTE published its £500m proposals to provide a Light Rapid Transport system embracing Birmingham, Coventry, Walsall and Wolverhampton. Greater Manchester PTE has plans for its own LRT network while Sheffield might also have such a system if the South Yorkshire PTE has its way. Meanwhile the 'daddy' of them all, the superlative Metro operated by the Tyne and Wear PTE, opened its final stretch of line to South Shields, so completing the £180m scheme. Meanwhile, in London LRT provided a wealth of news worthy of mention in this review, not the least of which was the repainting and restoration as far as practicable of a 1938 tube set to original condition. Such initiative brought LRT much public acclaim and thousands of pounds.

Below: The final 8-mile section of Tyne & Wear's Metro system, from Heworth to South Shields, was officially opened by Councillor Michael Campbell, Leader of Tyne & Wear County Council at a ceremony at Chichester on 23 March. The total cost of the Metro has been £180m and it carries over 160 000 passengers daily. Of the 88 twin railcars, 70 are required for the full daily service. Further expansion plans mooted by civic leaders are unlikely, though, for the government is unlikely to invest more money in view of the large amount previously allocated to this scheme. The first extension would be either to Newcastle airport or to Sunderland. This picture shows the re-opening special at Chichester station on the South Shields line on 23 March. *(Murray Brown)*

LRT round-up

Top: London Regional Transport's No 12 *Sarah Siddons* again took to BR metals and headed a public excursion from Waterloo to Portsmouth on 7 July. It ran via Effingham Junction and Guildford and returned to Victoria via the Mid Sussex line. *Sarah Siddons* also put in an appearance at the Eastleigh Open Day and hauled the green 4SUB to that event from Wimbledon. The railtour from Waterloo was titled 'The Mary Rose' and the ex-Metropolitan Railway veteran is seen passing Vauxhall. In 1984 came the remarkable revelation that the infamous diesel ban which prevents privately-owned machines from running on BR tracks also includes *Sara Siddons* and the 2BIL emu. Will these vintage machines run in 1985? Tune in to next year's 'Jane's Railway Year'! *(Peter Groom)*

Centre two: In March 1984 Highgate depot on the Northern Line was closed, having been run down for many years, and not having taken up its full role under the 1933-40 New Works Programme. The last two trains to enter the depot were formed of seven cars and are seen the the last day, 25 March. One of these 1959 sets had the honour of being the last off the depot and is pictured entering East Finchley station. As the year closed, the tracks and buildings at Highgate remained in mothballed condition pending a decision on their future. *(Both: Brian Hardy)*

Bottom: Bakerloo Line services were restored to Harrow & Wealdstone during peak hours only from 4 June. For two months previously, crew-training trips were worked during the midday period and one such train is pictured in the reversing siding at Harrow with a Class 501 dc emu passing on the up line. The Class 501 units enjoyed their last complete year in service in 1984, being due for replacement by 2EPB and Class 313 units from May 1985. *(Brian Hardy)*

Left: Engineering works of an emergency nature required the suspension of the Bakerloo Line service between Piccadilly and Waterloo on 19 May and during the Spring Bank Holiday weekend. This gave an unusual opportunity to use the 'Piccadilly' destination plates, as depicted here on a 1938 tube stock train at Queens Park. Trains of 1959 stock which also operate the Bakerloo Line do not have 'Piccadilly' blinds and generally showed 'special'. *(Brian Hardy)*

Right: In April 1984 all but two of the sleet locomotives on the Underground were scrapped. These were so converted in 1938-40 but first saw passenger service on the Central London Railway from 1903. No ESL114, illustrated here at Cockfosters on 23 April, two days before scrapping, was the last to remain in the old livery of unlined lake. *(Brian Hardy)*

Below: A rare event took place on 26 March when LRT borrowed from BR's Research & Development Division their 2-car Park Royal dmu for track recording purposes. The special is seen passing Croxley on the Watford branch of the Metropolitan. *(Brian Hardy)*

1938 stock restored

A delightful event took place in the autumn with the repainting in original livery of one of LRT's 1938 tube sets at Stonebridge Park depot. The initiative for this painting came from the depot staff and it duly gained approval from LRT's management. A 3- and 4-car set were painted in London Transport red, a darker shade than the present LT Bus Red, and considerable attention was paid to embellishments. These included provision of 'No Smoking' transfers (instead of 'Non Smoking'), station line diagrams in the original style but, of necessity, showing interchange with BR instead of the LMS! In addition the 'shovel' type lamp shades were re-instated, having been accumulated from around the LRT system. In a commendable example of business acumen, the advertising rights were sold to a West End theatrical agency which included promotions for the 'Starlight Express' musical. One of the driving vehicles is pictured at Stonebridge Park depot early in November. Note the original style numbering in gold, replacing the smaller white number.

Andy Gaylard applies the vertical cream stripes to one of the 1938 cars. The transfer reads 'Non Smoking' on the exterior and 'No Smoking' on the interior. The white LRT roundel has given way to the original 'London Transport' as seen here, also in gold. Such has been the approval of this initiative that it is hoped LRT will revert to this livery and lettering style for future builds. The repainting and associated work on these seven cars was supervised by Stonebridge Park's acting Depot Manager, Andy Barr. (Both: *Murray Brown*)

PRESERVATION

The preservation world followed a course similar to that taken in 1983 but the overall impression once again was one of accomplishment against many odds, notably the perennial problem of finance. With Barry scrapyard increasingly depleted, every year sees exiles from this yard lit up for the first time. The year under review again saw those interested in diesel traction saving their beloved machines, an achievement accompanied by strange emotions as most can remember these relative veterans brand new. The first Class 40s were saved as were some Class 127 dmus and, commendably, an example of the BTH Class 15. The year was also one to be remembered for the arrival of several immigrant locomotives. Two massive Beyer Garratt machines arrived from South Africa for preservation, as did three former Greek locomotives. BR paint schemes continued to find favour, with several old machines reappearing in BR colours and the restoration of two BR Standard locomotives which only ran in BR livery. The quest for line extensions was again pursued during the year with the Severn Valley Railway setting the yardstick, probably unattainable by anyone else, in raising well over the £300 000 in its share issue to fund the Kidderminster extension. Meanwhile, one of the most incredible preservation projects of them all continued to make progress in 1984 – *Duke of Gloucester* was reunited with its rebuilt cylinder . . .

Below: What has to be the surprise preservation event in 1984 was the announcement that Harvey's of Bristol, the famous sherry manufacturer, was to pay for and restore the derelict hulk of GWR 'King' No 6023 *King Edward II*. Harveys have secured the locomotive on behalf of the Brunel Engineering Centre where it will be the main item on display at the proposed Brunel Museum situated at Temple Meads station, Bristol. *King Edward II* is to be restored to working order, a formidable task bearing in mind one of the driving wheels has been cut by torch. The photograph depicts Harveys Managing Director David Beatty (centre) handling over the cheque for £21 000 to Michael Cockayne, Chairman of the King Edward II Preservation Society, which had the aim of restoring the 'King' to working order. In the light raincoat is Tony Byrne, Director of the Bristol Marketing Board. The cheque was handed over at Barry scrapyard, where the 'King' has reigned for 22 years. The 4-6-0 was delivered to Bristol by low loader on 23 December. *(Harveys of Bristol)*

SVR reaches Kidderminster

Above: One of the highlights of the preservation world in 1984 was the phenomenal raising of capital by means of a share issue by the Severn Valley Railway to finance its extension into Kidderminster. The SVR had set its target at £300 000 and this was fully subscribed in the first week of May only 24 weeks after being offered. As a result a further share issue was authorised. As a consequence of this success, work commenced immediately on the provision of a 1930-style GWR building for the SVR's Kidderminster terminus. The first SVR train to enter Kidderminster yard under SVR ownership was on 11 May when D1013 *Western Ranger* headed a pw train conveying concrete sleepers. *(G F Bannister)*

Below: Final preparations for the official opening the next day sees a last works train headed by preserved Class 08 No D3022, itself a new acquisition to the SVR in 1984, about to leave the new Kidderminster terminus on 29 July. *(Hugh Ballantyne)*

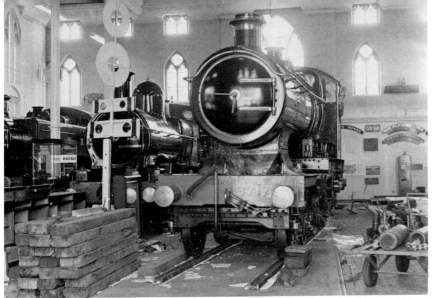

Left: One of the star attractions (but regrettably not a real 'Star') for the GWR 150 celebrations is the famous 4-4-0 No 3717 *City of Truro*. Its appearance at the junketings means that this locomotive will hold a remarkable record, that of having twice left a museum to be put into working order, *City of Truro* entered Swindon Museum on 15 April 1962 after earlier having been restored to working order to work specials between the years 1957-1961. Twenty-two years later, on 10 July 1984, the 4-4-0 was winched out to be taken by transporter to the Civil Engineer's yard at Swindon where it was inspected before haulage to the Severn Valley Railway for boiler overhaul. Pictured about to emerge for the second time from Swindon Museum, No 3717 was slewed towards the main entrance in preparation for the great adventure. *(Hugh Ballantyne)*

Above: The journey from Swindon to the Severn Valley Railway took place on 14 July and Class 37 No 37304 provided the power. Here the cavalcade is seen crossing onto the SVR from BR at Kidderminster. *(Hugh Ballantyne)*

City of Truro leaves Swindon

Left: No 3717 is seen waiting its turn for boiler attention at Bridgnorth on 23 August. It was expected that the remedial work would cost in the region of £30 000 and *City of Truro* would be outshopped bearing its original number 3440. The locomotive was hydraulically tested on 30 August when several tubes leaked thus dashing hopes that the engine could be steamed with its existing tubes. *(Mick Roberts)*

Festival line comes and goes

Below: With the River Mersey as a backdrop, the R&ER's *River Irt* heads a train on the circuit on 30 June. Besides *River Irt*, other R&ER power used for the railway were diesel locomotives *Shelagh of Eskdale* and the 'Silver Jubilee' railcar set, while from the RH&DR came *The Bug, Black Prince* and *Samson*. *(Tom Heavyside)*

For the 1984 Liverpool International Garden Festival, a 2½-mile 15″ gauge railway was constructed amidst the many gardens, with motive power supplied by the Romney, Hythe & Dymchurch Railway and the Ravenglass & Eskdale Railway. The railway ran for six months until 14 October, after which the layout was dismantled. These six pictures illustrate one of the highlights of the 1984 railway year.

Right: RH&DR No 6 *Samson* is dwarfed by a full-sized headboard at Fulwood station on 2 September. The Garden Festival Railway carried HM the Queen, Prince Philip, Princess Margaret and other Royal Family members during its six-month season. *(Peter Groom)*

Opposite:
The Garden Festival Railway was laid out in a large loop with a branch to the main Festival entrance. There were six stations in total and trains took approximately twenty minutes to complete the circuit. In this picture the 'Silver Jubilee' railcar pauses in Festival Hall station on 30 June. *(Tom Heavyside)*

Below: Samson gallops away downgrade from Mill station on 25 August heading towards Festival Hall station. Up to three trains could be accommodated on the circuit at one time and the line was equipped with colour light signals operated by track circuits. *(Colin Boocock)*

Right: Shelagh of Eskdale was usually the relief locomotive and is seen on 25 August between Dingle station and the main entrance. The coaching stock fleet comprised 26 vehicles. Of these twenty were new toast rack vehicles built by Steamtown Carnforth whilst six were loaned from the RH&DR. *(Colin Boocock)*

Opposite:
On 25 August, RH&DR 4-6-2 No 11 *Black Prince* hammers hard upgrade out of the tunnel near Dingle station. A total of eleven men made up the railway's operating complement. *(Colin Boocock)*

Left and centre: Celebrated Class A4 No 4498 *Sir Nigel Gresley* returned to the steam scene in 1984 after an absence of 18 months during which time its boiler underwent the statutory 7-year overhaul ordained by BR. The boiler was reunited with the frames on 28 January and No 4498 was steam tested on 26 March. *Sir Nigel Gresley* moved again under its own power on 28 May but, sadly, A4 Locomotive Society Limited officials refused to bow to public demand and return the A4 to steam in BR livery as No 60007. This would have been a golden opportunity to give *Sir Nigel* a new impetus and focus attention on it but it was not to be and No 60009's summer visit from its Scottish home stole the limelight in 1984. *Sir Nigel* made its first main line run on 9 June when it worked 'The Clitheronian' from, would you believe, Clitheroe to York. Another of No 4498's moments in 1984 was its exhibition at the 1984 Doncaster Works Open Day on 29 July. No 60009 *Union of South Africa* poses next to what could have been No 60007 but is still No 4498, outside the Paint Shop at Doncaster Works on 27 July. *(Jim Coleman (top); David Wilcock (centre))*

Below: A welcome machine to return to steam on 1 April was the 'Black Five' on the North Yorkshire Moors Railway, No 45428 *Eric Treacy*. The locomotive last turned a wheel in 1975 but progress could not be made for several years as no commitment could be obtained from its owner as to where the locomotive would be based. Having resolved this matter, the NYMR fully overhauled the 4-6-0 and, as a finishing touch, restored its BR number, the 'Black Five' having previously carried No 5428. Sadly, as seems to have befallen NYMR locomotives in recent years, a serious failure occurred when the right hand valve seized and the locomotive was withdrawn for extensive remedial treatment on 23 August after having covered 6549 miles. In this picture it is raising steam in the company of K1 No 62005 at Grosmont on 22 April. *(Mick Roberts)*

Engines overhauled

Above: The Standard 4 Preservation Group's 2-6-0 No 76017 was placed in traffic for the first time after complete overhaul on 19 May on its home line, the Mid Hants Railway. No 76017 was purchased from Barry scrapyard and was initially taken in January 1974 to the Quainton Railway Centre. In 1978 it was moved to the Mid Hants line for restoration at Ropley, where it was photographed in steam on the day of its return to service. *(Mick Roberts)*

Standard double

Left: BR Standard 4-6-0 No 75069 was returned to steam on the Severn Valley Railway in 1984. It was the 37th locomotive to be retrieved from Barry scrapyard and was moved to the SVR in 1973. No 75069's overhaul cost £30 000. It was lit up for the first time on 30 July and the 4-6-0 moved under its own power the following day after 18 years of inactivity. It made its passenger debut on 17 August when it double-headed with No 3205 on the 1140 Bridgnorth-Kidderminster. Just a few hours into the new year on 1 January 1985 75069 is seen leaving Arley. *(David C Rogers)*

Two for the price of one

Above: Railway photographer Peter Zabek has a penchant shared by many of today's enthusiasts for locomotives to carry BR livery. In 1984 it was the turn of the North Eastern Locomotive Preservation Group's Class K1 No 2005 to receive his attention when, for one season only, it was painted in BR black livery and number at Peter's expense. NELPG had earlier conducted a ballot amongst its members, who voted to retain the LNER Apple Green livery following its overhaul during the winter of 1984/85. Four volunteers, including the photographer, put No 2005 into its correct colour (it never carried LNER number or green livery) and their efforts are seen to effect in this magnificent scene as No 62005, complete with authentic shedcode and 'blood and custard' coaches, reaches Ellerbeck Summit on 12 August. *(Peter J Robinson)*

Below: It was suggested in 1984 that NELPG's Class K1 should be one of the locomotives rostered to work the Fort William-Mallaig summer services in 1985. With this in mind and as a pleasant and amusing diversion, NELPG disguised No 62005 as one of the late-lamented Fort William-allocated K1s, No 62052. It ran in this state for the first week in September prior to being withdrawn from traffic on 7 September for major overhaul. Bearing a 65J shedplate and inscribed bufferbeam, No '62052' alias 62005, alias 2005 leaves Goathland with a Pickering train on 2 September. *(Hugh Ballantyne)*

Two 0-6-2Ts

Above: The Horsehay Steam Trust's Class 56XX 0-6-2T No 5619 from 27 May began to work on passenger trains over its 500-yard length of line. Until then the locomotive had been steamed for special events but did not work trains. This picture shows the unlined GWR green tank returning to Horsehay from Heath Hill tunnel on the former Horsehay-Lightmoore line on 26 August. The Mk 1 coach is the unique LFK (Lounge First Corridor) No 14901 obtained from the Severn Valley Railway and the GWR 'Toad' brake van is No 17453. *(Hugh Ballantyne)*

Below: The 64th locomotive to leave Barry scrapyard was Class 56XX No 6619 and in 1974 it left to find a somewhat strange home on the North Yorkshire Moors Railway. Restoration started in earnest in 1979 when it was purchased by Peter Proud and Kevin Gould, and their efforts were rewarded in October 1984 when No 6619 moved under steam, for the first time. The quote of the year comes from Kevin Gould who commented, "She runs like a Rolls-Royce and so she should – we could have bought one with what we have spent on 6619!"
These pictures show this incongruous machine which is widely expected to be the most suitable locomotive to work on the Moors line raising steam on 14 October during its running-in trials. The location is Grosmont shed. *(Both: Mick Roberts)*

Odyssey from Greece

Right

After six years of negotiations, the Mid Hants Railway finally received from Greece two former Hellenic State Railway locomotives, Baldwin S160 No 575 and North British WD No 951. They arrived, together with a third locomotive, Class LB No 960 which was destined for the newly formed Lavender Line in East Sussex, aboard the Greek vessel *Empros* at Ipswich and were unloaded on 28 August. This remarkable picture shows the three locomotives in the hold of the freighter, Nos 960 (left), 575 (centre) and 951 (right) before unloading at the Cliff Quay, Ipswich Docks. *(Mick Roberts)*

Below

No 575 is lowered onto the road transporter for its journey to the Mid Hants Railway. No 575 was US Army Transportation Corps No 3278 built by Alco, works number 71533/1944, but carries the boiler from Baldwin 70340/1944 (TC No 3383). The plan is to paint this locomotive in Longmoor Military Railway blue as No 701. No 575 is a similar locomotive to K&WVR-based 2-8-0 No 5820 'Big Jim'. *(Mick Roberts)*

Opposite

Top left

Hellenic (OSE) Class LB 2-10-0 No 960 emerges from the hold of the *Empros*. The locomotive was built by the North British Co Ltd in January 1944, works number 25458. It became WD No 3672 (later 73672) and will now be restored to running order in Southern Railway green and used for special occasions on David Milham's Lavender Line at Isfield. This locomotive is the only oil burner of the three and was originally intended to be one of the three locomotives bought by the Mid Hants Railway. As a result of rising costs, it was offered to David Milham for his railway as the Greek authorities directed that the sale would apply to all three or nothing. *(Mick Roberts)*

Top right and bottom

No 951 is pictured being lifted onto terra firma at Ipswich on 27 August and, later, on 22 September at Ropley shed on the Mid Hants Railway, where it will be restored in BR livery and carry the number 90775. This is because it is from the same build of locomotives which ran in BR service carrying the number range 90750-90774. It is planned to remove the air pump. *(Both: Mick Roberts)*

Tanks back in steam

Above: Back in steam on the Kent & East Sussex Railway in 1984 was London, Brighton & South Coast Railway Class A1X 'Terrier' No 10 *Sutton* after a two-year overhaul costing £15 000. It returned to active service on 29 May. This diminutive 0-6-0T leads an evening freight into Rolvenden from Tenterden on 3 June. *(Peter Groom)*

Above: Paint it black! This highly popular theme continued unabated in 1984 and many people were made happy on the Bluebell Railway when the North London Railway 0-6-0T was outshopped in BR livery and numbered 58850. It had received an extensive overhaul and is seen heading down Freshfield bank to Sheffield Park on 22 July. *(Rodney Lissenden)*

Below: After a nine year restoration, BR built 0-6-0ST No 9681 was steamed for the first time at its home on the Dean Forest Railway. It made its public debut on 30 September sporting BR black livery and 88A shed plate. No 9681 left Barry scrapyard on 10 October 1975 and was the 75th locomotive to be rescued from this steam valhalla. It is particularly noteworthy that this pannier tank was restored with practically no facilities in poor working conditions. This picture of No 9681 reborn is dated 21 October when it was working weekend trains at Norchard. *(Peter J Skelton)*

Welcome to the Lavender Line

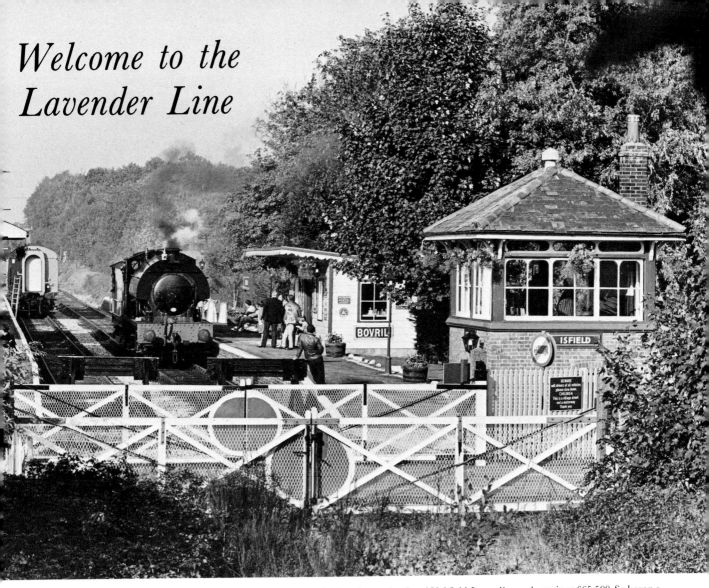

Above: On 16 June 1983 David and Gwen Milham became owners of Isfield station on the closed Uckfield-Lewes line – a bargain at £65 500. So began a remarkable adventure which resulted in a new railway centre, the Lavender Line, being born and, indeed, opened in 1984. The line is named after coal merchant A E Lavender & Sons, who operated out of the station's goods yard. The enormous transformation of the overgrown and derelict site was a mammoth task and has encompassed the renovation of the signal box, restoration of the main booking hall building, the building of a replica waiting room (the Bluebell Railway has the original) and the laying of track. The plan of the owners is to provide a high quality wine and dine service and the track will initially be extended about one mile northwards towards Uckfield. This picture shows the beautifully restored Isfield station from the southern (Lewes) end with RSH-built 'Ugly' 0-6-0ST No 62 giving rides to passengers in a GWR 'Toad' brake van No 17455 on 23 September. *(Mick Roberts)*

Below: This view of Isfield station is taken from the north end and shows the Greek 2-10-0 No 960, which was delivered on 30 August. The stock comprises Pullman coach *Sapphire*, which was obtained from the Ashford Steam Centre, Mk 1s TSO No E4668 and FO No E3125 from Stour Valley line, and the unique Lounge Buffet car No E1883 which, too, arrived from the Stour Valley in August. Besides 'Ugly' No 62, the Lavender Line has Barclay 0-4-0ST No 945 *Annie*, the first locomotive to arrive on the site on 23 February. *(Mick Roberts)*

Saved from the torch

Above: Peter Sansom, who purchased Class 55 No 55015 *Tulyar*, took it to the Midland Railway Centre at Butterley in 1984. This locomotive had been at Derby following purchase where it had undergone bogie tests on behalf of the Research & Development Division. Because the Deltic had been static and exposed to the elements for so long since the Spring of 1982, there was a good deal of work required before *Tulyar* provided the music for which it was famed. Sporting a reminder of one of its most memorable journeys, No 55015 sits in the platform at Butterley on 23 September during an Open Weekend to celebrate the 25th anniversary of No D4 *Great Gable*. *(Michael Jacob)*

Centre: The luckiest Deltic of them all: that was the title given to No 55016 *Gordon Highlander* when it was purchased for preservation by the 9000 Locomotive Ltd. Its survival was due solely to the fact that it was the final Deltic in the scrapping line and lasted long enough for interest to be generated. Although it was initially bought as a source of spares for No 9000 *Royal Scots Grey*, closer examination revealed that, despite the missing parts and vandalised cabs, it was deemed capable of being restored in its own right. No 55016 was towed to the Nene Valley Railway on 23 July with sister stablemate No 9000, which had been a visitor to the Doncaster Works Open Day on 22 July. Work immediately commenced with smartening up the derelict looking No 55016 at Wansford in preparation, expected in 1985, for a start-up! On 11 March this 3¼-million miles traveller was pictured in Doncaster works pondering a better future. *(Gary Grafton)*

Left: On the evening of 17 February the Class 40 Preservation Society's locomotive, No 40145, was delivered to the East Lancashire Railway Preservation Society's headquarters at Bury Transport Museum. No 40145 had been condemned in 1983 following a derailment at Stourton, Leeds and had been stabled at Crewe pending preservation or scrap. The CFPS had bought No 40145 minus air brake equipment and the remainder of 1984 was spent reconnecting the brake system which had been rendered inoperative with the removal of the air brake components. A ballot conducted by CFPS members voted to return No 40145 to its original green livery with small yellow warning panel. In this picture, the former star performer of the 'Queen of Scots' Pullman when the locomotive was based new at Neville Hill, Leeds, is hauled by the Bury Transport Museum from Buckley Wells, to which point a Class 25 had hauled the 'Whistler' from Crewe. *(Richard Fox)*

Above: A new arrival on the Mid Hants Railway in 1984 was Class 08 shunter No 08288, formerly D3358. It made the news when, despicably, it was sabotaged while at Farnham en route to the preserved line. Wiring was damaged and sand was poured into the sump. Luckily, the damage is not irreparable. Here, No 08288 is seen at Farnham, scene of the incident, on 15 September. *(I C Scotchman)*

Above: Salvation came to one of Britain's less successful diesel classes in 1984 when the Class 15 Preservation Society secured pre-heat Departmental unit No ADB 968001 on 18 July. The locomotive had been awaiting scrap at Healey Mills following no bids when it was offered for sale by tender. After its purchase, the Class 15 Preservation Society had obtained permission to take the locomotive to the Peak Railway but this agreement was suddenly rescinded and a new home was sought. Both the North Yorkshire Moors Railway and the West Somerset Railway offered a home, but as the transport costs were prohibitive at that time, the Class 15 was taken on 4 November by road to the South Yorkshire Railway Preservation Society's premises at Chapeltown. The photograph shows the 1960-built veteran shortly after arrival. The owners plan to purchase traction motors similar to those removed by BR from the Irish Railways, Coras Iompair Eirann. *(Les Nixon)*

Left: Two Class 08 shunters were purchased by the North Staffordshire Railway based at Cheddleton during 1984. These were Nos 08350 and 08359 and were brought from Swindon. The shunters were delivered by road transporter on 18 September (08350) and 20 September (08359) and the photograph depicts No 08350 being delivered to its new home. *(D P Cawthorn)*

Below: The demise of the Class 127 dmus early in the year had been awaited by some of the preservation fraternity, for this class is one of the few which does not contain blue asbestos insulation. Both the Great Central Railway and the Torbay & Dartmouth Railway acquired examples of the class, but as BR removed the intermediate trailer cars for further use, replacing blue asbestos lined trailer cars, the T&DR bought two Class 116 trailer cars to insert in the formation. The dmu vehicles bought by the T&DR were Nos M51592 and M51604 (Class 127) and M59003 and M59004 (Class 116). They are pictured on 19 February at Goodrington BR sidings after arrival from Tyseley. *(Roger Penny)*

Above: A Light Railway Order was granted to the East Somerset Railway to permit it to extend to Mendip Vale, and track laying was then put in hand in preparation for passenger services to begin. In this picture Austerity 0-6-0ST No 68005 (not the genuine BR 68005) is in charge of a freight train at Mendip Vale on 6 October. *(David Wilcock)*

Route extensions

Right: The Nene Valley Railway launched a £185 000 appeal to raise funds to relay the 1½ miles from its boundary with BR, Longueville Junction, into the NVR's new terminus in the city to be called Peterborough Nene Valley. Lord Gretton conducted the ceremony on 2 May when the appeal was launched and the occasion was marked by the lifting into position of a section of silver-painted rail by members of the Peterborough Rugby Club. Here the lifting is underway, supervised by England Rugby Union Captain Peter Wheeler, while Standard Class 5 4-6-0 No 73050 looks on. *(NVR)*

Above: It is now an accepted fact of life for the major private railways to entertain visiting locomotives as an added attraction. 1984 on the Severn Valley Railway saw the Great Western Society's Castle No 5051 spend four weeks on this popular line. Here *Drysllwyn Castle* is seen near Sterns on 30 September with the 1218 Kidderminster-Bridgnorth. *(Hugh Ballantyne)*

Right: The Kent & East Sussex Railway celebrated its 10th anniversary in 1984 and, as part of the junketings, the Great Western Society's 0-4-2T No 1466 paid a brief visit to the line as an added attraction. The locomotive is pictured on the bank up to Tenterden before working the first train of the day on 10 June. No 1466 returned to its Didcot home after this last day of working. *(Peter Groom)*

Pastures new

Right: Standard Class 4MT 2-6-4T No 80064 found a new permanent home in 1984 when it was moved from the Torbay & Dartmouth Railway to the Bluebell Railway following a dispute between the owners and the management of the T&DR. No 80064 worked its first Bluebell train on 17 June. Approaching Horsted Keynes on 26 December, No 80064 is powering the 1520 train from Sheffield Park. *(Mick Roberts)*

Garratt homecoming

1984 was the year of the immigrant Garratts, for two of these awe-inspiring machines reached these shores. The first was the welcome return to Manchester of Gorton-built Beyer Peacock GL Class No 2352 from the South African Railways (SAR). The Greater Manchester Museum of Science and Industry took delivery of the two tenders on 31 January and the boiler and cab section on 2 February. It was donated to the museum by SAR and was a personal triumph for Dr Richard Hills, Curator of the Museum (pictured here with No 2352 at Liverpool Road on 14 February). It is to be restored as a static exhibit in black livery. The general view was taken on 1 July. *(Richard Fox; Hugh Ballantyne)*

Above: "Please can we have one of your Garratts?". So asked Peter Pratt of the Plym Valley Railway-based society, 4160 Ltd, to the South African Railways (SAR). Three years later 160-ton 1957-built Garratt Class No 4112 arrived free of transport costs on board the container ship *S A Sederberg*, courtesy of OCL Ltd. The 3 ft 6 in gauge giant was photographed at Marsh Mills on the Plym Valley Railway on 24 October. As a gesture of thanks to the SAR authorities, the locomotive was named *Springbok* at a ceremony on 1 August. It is planned to run the Garratt on a short length of track and in the long term operate it on mixed gauge. Can you see BR giving away D200? *(Hugh Ballantyne)*

Below: An idea of the size of this mammoth machine can be gleaned with this view of No 4112. The locomotive arrived in this country on 23 July and was unloaded from the container ship *S A Sederberg* in four sections. Although the locomotive was donated and transported free of charge, there was a bill of £20 000 to pay in respect of dock loading and road transport charges. *(Roger Penny)*

Progress at Buxton

Top: 21 April was a historic day for Peak Rail, for on that day passengers were able to be entertained on the Buxton station line, which runs for 150 yards. Whilst this length is modest, further expansion can only be achieved if the Bridge Street overbridge can be reinstated. Then progress can be made towards establishing a service to Ashwood Dale. The final major hurdle was crossed by Peak Rail on 13 June when Derbyshire County Council gave permission for the section between Matlock and Rowsley to be used as a railway. This agreement thus gave PR permission to relay track throughout from Matlock to Buxton. 0-6-0ST *Brookes No 1* officiated at the opening ceremony at Buxton and is seen breaking the tape to commence passenger operation. *(Brian Cuttell)*

. . . Bury . .

On 22 May the East Lancashire Railway Preservation Society received into its care at the Bury Transport Museum 'Black Five' No 45337. The locomotive arrived at Bury by road from Barry scrapyard and is owned by the 26B Railway Company Ltd. It is seen outside its new home after arrival from South Wales. *(Richard Fox)*

. . . and Butterley

Left: There was considerable building activity at the Midland Railway Centre in 1984. At Swanwick Junction a start was made on the re-erection of a large shed obtained from an engineering company which is to house the MRC's museum collection. It was pictured under construction on 22 April. Meanwhile, at Butterley the former station building from Whitwell in North Derbyshire was re-erected and opened for public use in the spring of 1984. This photograph is also dated 22 April. *(Both: Brian Cuttell)*

Halls of fame

Sticklers for authenticity, the Severn Valley Railway corrected an inaccuracy by placing their two 'Halls' into service duly repainted in correct period liveries but also by fitting them with correct period tenders. These latter had previously been unavailable for operating reasons. On 29 September No 4930 *Hagley Hall*, sporting a Collett tender with the GWR roundel of the 1930s, picks up speed near Sterns with the 1548 Kidderminster-Bridgnorth train. A day later No 6960 *Raveningham Hall*, now carrying a Hawksworth tender painted in the first BR livery, approaches Sterns with the 1140 from Bridgnorth. With the efforts made to pay attention to such detail, it is surprising that No 6960 has been fitted with a non-standard smokebox door numberplate. *(Both: Hugh Ballantyne)*

Narrow gauge novelties

Left: HRH Prince Michael of Kent officially opened the museum complex at the Amberley Chalk Pits in West Sussex on 5 June. Seen here on 10 June are Bagnall locomotives *Wendy* (2091/1919) (on loan from Dursley Light Railway) and *Polar Bear* (1781/1905) at the Brockham terminus. *(Mick Roberts)*

Below: Former Dinorwic Slate Quarries 0-4-0ST *Jerry M* was restored to working order over a 14-year period, including a completely new boiler, and was steamed for the first time in April. It is seen here on the Hollycombe Woodland Railway, Liphook in Hampshire on 10 June. *(Mick Roberts)*

Right: There have been changes on the Fairbourne Railway in North Wales in 1984. The line changed ownership with Dr Sidney Ellerton, Mr John Ellerton and Mr John Milner assuming control. This famous narrow gauge line is to become narrower, for its present 15 in gauge is to be reduced to 12¼ in. Pictured on 18 June is 2-4-2 No 362 *Sydney* running round its train at Barmouth Ferry. This locomotive is a rebuild of *Sian* (Guest 18/63). At the time of this picture, stock from the ill-fated French narrow gauge line Réseau Guerledan had arrived at Fairbourne and this will be used when the new gauge is installed. *(Peter Groom)*

Permanent way relaying work on the Groundle Glen narrow gauge railway in the Isle of Man had reached half way by the date of this photograph, 25 March, leaving only 350 yards or so to complete. Services using diesel locomotives commenced during the summer for the first time since 1962. The rolling stock, two diesel locomotives and track materials were all acquired from Doddington House in Avon, a stately home project which had gone into liquidation during 1983. *(Mick Roberts)*

Hudson-Hunslet diesel locomotive No 4395 of 1952 shunts an engineering train on the Groundle Glen Railway in the Isle of Man during track clearance and relaying operations on 25 March. *(Mick Roberts)*

Third rail developments

Above and left:
One of the most surprising events of the year took place on 23 September when the National Railway Museum's preserved 2-BIL unit No 2090 was allowed onto BR metals with an advertised excursion. What is so remarkable is that the ban operated by BR in respect of preserved diesels also includes electric traction and yet this tour, to quote third rail parlance, short-circuited the ban. Coupled with the 2-BIL unit was the 'preserved' 4-SUB No 4732. This unit is in a strange state of limbo for it still belongs to BR and is officially withdrawn. It shares the same status as Class 40 No 40122, alias D200, in being retained for commercial reasons. The tour, organised by the Southern Electric Group and the Locomotive Club of Great Britain, was appropriately titled 'The Electric Phoenix' in view of the fact that unit No 2090 had not run previously with passengers on the main line. Prior to its run, a test trip was undertaken from Brighton with BR staff and their families being offered a run in this unit. Starting and finishing at Brighton, the SEG/LCGB tour covered various Southern lines including a visit to Waterloo. In these pictures, the 2-BIL is seen with the 4-SUB behind it at Eastbourne and also at Brighton at the conclusion of the railtour. (Both: *Alex Dasi-Sutton)*

Left: A disgraceful act of vandalism took place on 15 August when the centre trailer car from the only surviving 4-DD double-decker emu Unit No 4002 was broken up by a scrap contractor at Ashford. The destination of vehicle No S13503 was the last act in a long-running dispute between BR and the owner of the 4-DD unit which had prevented BR from clearing the Ashford site, formerly the location of the Ashford Steam Centre. Despite a court ruling, no progress could be made and even though the BR Property Board wanted to see this unit kept intact in view of its uniqueness, the owner actually decreed that the individual vehicles should not be sold to preservationists. And so the scrap contractors were brought in. No sooner had the trailer vehicle (and a fireless steam locomotive) been reduced to scrap, than the two driving vehicles, Nos S13003 and S13004 were, in the end, privately sold. No S13004 was temporarily taken to a Woolwich scrapyard and thence to a warehouse in Woolwich where it is seen being moved in on 21 October. This vehicle was later moved to the Northants Steam Centre. *(David S Morris)*

On 1 August the Kent & East Sussex Railway's 0-6-0T 'Terrier' No 3 *Bodiam* hauled its first passenger train after overhaul and repainting in BR livery as No 32670. This 'Terrier' also at one time carried the number 70 and was named *Poplar*. The diminutive Class A1X is seen climbing the bank approaching Tenterden with a mixed train from Wittersham Road on the last day of the season, 25 November. *(Mick Roberts)*

Terrier return

Green engine contrasts

Above: The Bluebell Railway's West Country Pacific No 34023 *Blackmore Vale* was repainted temporarily in early BR-Style Brunswick green for the 1984 season, but was rarely used because of the coal strike. The locomotive, seen here entering Horsted Keynes on 2 September, is correctly bereft of the crests which had been added to honour the memory of its designer, O V S Bulleid. *(Mick Roberts)*

Below: 1984 saw preservation of first examples of the English Electric Class 40s. No 40106, the only 40 to remain green throughout its BR career, was acquired by Gerald Boden and entered service officially on the Great Central Railway on the weekend of 11/12 August. Prior to its return to passenger duties, this 'Whistler' received the name *Atlantic Conveyor* at a ceremony at Loughborough on 9 August when John Brocklehurst, Second Officer of the original *Atlantic Conveyor* vessel lost in the Falklands confrontation with the loss of nine crew members, unveiled the nameplate. For once, the practice of bestowing a nameplate on a locomotive which has never carried one, usually frowned upon by enthusiasts, was met with full approval for the *Atlantic Conveyor* nameplates had been manufactured in the style of the original named LMR-allocated Class 40s which carried 'Liner' names. David Newton, who manufactures many of BR's nameplates, provided those for *Atlantic Conveyor*. Carrying a headboard, the significance of which was that No 40106 was the first of its Class to enter active preservation, No 40106 glistens in the afternoon sun while departing from Loughborough with the last train of the day for Rothley on 12 August. *(Mick Roberts)*

Diesels rejuvenated

Above: On 2 April 1981 the Western Locomotive Association's Class 52 No D1062 *Western Courier* suffered a serious power unit failure which was to see the locomotive out of action for three years. During this time a replacement power unit was rebuilt and extensive body repairs and repaint undertaken on D1062. The WLA's pride and joy finally moved again under its own power on 19 May. *Western Courier* together with *Western Ranger* were playing to the gallery on 6/7 October during the SVR's 'Western Weekend' and D1062, still awaiting the fitting of name and numberplates, is pictured approaching Eardington with the 1510 Bridgnorth-Kidderminster on 6 October. *(Hugh Ballantyne)*

Below: The Diesel & Electric Group's Class 14 No D9526 was successfully started over the weekend of 17/18 March following extensive overhaul. It is believed it last ran under its own power in 1976. No D9526 had a proving run on the West Somerset Railway on 29 March and hauled its first train on 15 July when it partook in a ceremony at which it was handed over by Mr E D Knights, Manager of Blue Circle Cement Company, the locomotive's former owner. D9526 joined the D&EG's other Class 14 No D9551 for service duties and the pair are seen on a Bishops Lydeard train at Combe Florey on 7 October. *(Roger Penny)*

Right: The private group of shareholders at the Bury Transport Museum, who had purchased Class 24 Departmental unit ADB 968009 in 1983 from March depot, achieved a significant achievement in the spring of 1984 when the locomotive moved under its own power for the first time since purchase and, indeed, the first time since it was first converted on the Western Region to a Departmental unit. The traction motors were left intact on conversion, but much of the cabling and electrical gear was missing. Only when the locomotive was capable of moving itself did the owners allow the locomotive to discard its departmental number and have No 24054 duly reinstated. This picture shows the Class 24 shunting at Bury on 1 April. *(Stephen Willetts)*

Coaching stock round-up

Right: The 6-wheeled vehicle on BR is now a rarity and their ranks were depleted by one in 1984 when ADB 975249 was sold to the D4 *Great Gable* organisation based at Butterley. This vehicle, a Stove R, was formerly a BGZ No M32998 and was latterly used in the Tinsley breakdown train. Surrounded by appropriate LMS atmosphere, this vintage 6-wheeler is pictured at Butterley on 22 April. *(Brian Cuttell)*

Left: The Scottish Railway Preservation Society is no stranger to running tours with its own registered stock and 1984 saw the SRPS inaugurate their own Restaurant Miniature Buffet (RMB), as their Gresley Buffet is in need of remedial attention. The RMB is the former SC1866 and was sponsored by the whisky firm, Maclays. The SRPS do not own the Commonwealth bogies, these remaining the property of BR. It is seen in the formation of a SRPS Ayr-Mallaig railtour passing Cowlairs carriage sidings on 4 August. To the left of the RMB is the last Eastern Region RKB No E1513 which spent most of 1984 on loan to the SRPS. This vehicle has blue asbestos insulation, but as it is through wired for electric train heat, it can be used in eth formations if required. *(Tom Noble)*

Left: Trains For Pleasure, the organisation formed in 1983 to provide a rake of good quality Mk 1 vehicles for charter work, ran its first tour in 1984. The formation included the first two of its nine vehicles registered for main line running, FKs Nos E13317 and E13323. The tour ran from Butterley to Newcastle and return via the Settle & Carlisle line on 25 February. Here, Class 45/1 No 45103 tops Ais Gill summit with the cleaner TFP vehicles behind the locomotive. *(Bill Sharman)*

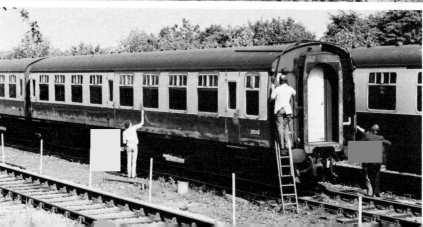

Below: TFP's nine vehicles (4 SKs, 2 FKs, 1 RMB, 1 TSO and 1 BCK) are kept on the Midland Railway Centre's site at Butterley under an arrangement whereby the MRT has the use of the vehicles for its own services in return for permitting TFP to stable them on its site. Work progressed during the year preparing the remaining TFP vehicles for registration but, as the year ended, the venture appeared to be in jeopardy due to the exhorbitant prices levied by BR for running a tour using TFP vehicles alone. The prices quoted were such that it would be cheaper for a tour operator to use BR-owned stock (which, ironically it does not have) than to use the TFP rake. This picture shows SK No E26049 being prepared for painting in maroon livery at Swanwick Junction on 17 June. *(John Tuffs)*

STEAM ON BR

Whilst 1984 saw no 'new' steam locomotives added to the approved list – an indication, perhaps, of why patronage took a dramatic turn for the worse on many steam specials – the year did see some notable innovations, particularly the return to steam haulage on the West Highland extension. The view that the remote location of this outpost for steam may have had a disappointing affect on passenger loadings was completely dispelled.

Two of the most popular machines, *Sir Nigel Gresley* and *Clan Line*, returned to traffic after major refits but for many the highlight of the year was the welcome return to England of John Cameron's Class A4 No 60009 *Union of South Africa*. With a pathetically short programme of tours, it was a resounding success and this acclaimed machine also put up some memorable performances in the process.

With prices of steam tours escalating beyond the pockets of many punters and the obvious need to introduce more varied traction and routes, 1984 has to be regarded as a pointer and a warning for the future prosperity of steam on BR. In this respect, previous reluctance to entertain steam on routes crying out for such attention was clearly in need of a further consideration.

Flying Scotsman, Sir Nigel Gresley and a reliveried Western Region HST were used in a new BR promotional television commercial which was filmed on the Hellified to Blackburn line from 30 October to 3 November. The HST was lettered 'Our trains now travel a distance equivalent of going round the world twenty-two times a day'. The steam-hauled train, comprising two Pullman vehicles, was lettered 'Well, I'll be blowed!' Filming took place with full possession of both tracks of the line, as the trains travelled in the same direction. Here *Flying Scotsman* and the HST perform for the cameras on board a helicopter near Newsholme on 1 November. *(John Macintosh)*

Scotsman comes to town

Below: In readiness for No 4472's Royal task it was considered prudent to have a test run down the Woolwich branch and for this purpose *Flying Scotsman* ran from Stratford to Woolwich on 19 November with two vehicles and Class 31 No 31223 at the rear. The photograph shows the cavalcade at West Ham station. *(John Titlow)*

A steam highlight of 1984 was the provision of the grand old lady herself, No 4472 *Flying Scotsman*, to haul the Royal train conveying HM The Queen Mother to North Woolwich to open the Great Eastern Railway Museum, also known as the Passmore Edwards Museum, on 20 November. This event produced a further novelty, for to bring the locomotive to the capital it was rostered to work 'The Fenman' railtour from Manchester to Spalding via the Midland main line, Nottingham and Sleaford. This train ran on 10 November and returned on 24 November. It was a little obvious that all those who have unsuccessfully campaigned for steam traction to run in the Eastern Counties have been vindicated for, contrary to the official line, steam in East Anglia is a feasible proposition. Indeed, the possibility emerged that 'The Fenman' might become an occasional occurrence.

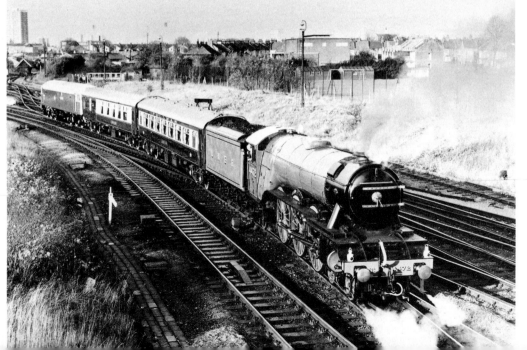

Left: No 4472 was adorned with a white cab roof in true Stratford tradition for its Royal run to Woolwich. On the red letter day, the A3 hauled two vehicles, a Pullman and a BCK both belonging to Pullmanrail, and the Queen Mother travelled in the train from Stratford Low Level to North Woolwich, where she first 'cabbed' the second most popular lady in the country before officially opening the Passmore Edwards Museum at North Woolwich station. After the visit, the Queen Mother returned to her residence by road whilst No 4472 and its train reversed to Stratford headed by specially repainted Class 47/4 No 47581 *Great Eastern*. Here *Flying Scotsman* is towed off Stratford depot into Temple Mills yard by the spotless Class 47 on 20 November. *(John Titlow)*

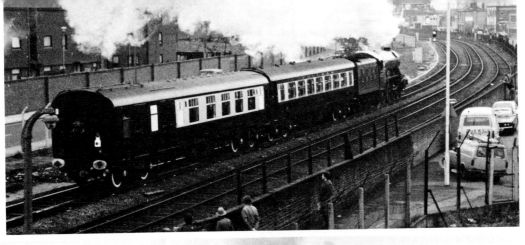

Left: On a murky 20 November No 4472 proceeds in stately fashion on its Royal journey at Canning Town en route to North Woolwich. *(Ian Cowley)*

Centre: Steam returned to the East Coast Main Line albeit briefly on 24 November when *Flying Scotsman* made its way from March to Spalding. There it took over 'The Fenman' railtour which took it back to home territory. Setting foot on its old stamping ground, the A3 is seen at Peterborough, from where it followed the ECML as far as Werrington Junction and on to Spalding. *(Michael J Collins)*

Below: Is there really any other locomotive in the country which can put this perfection of visual and auditory entertainment in the shade? The A3 is pictured on 24 November in charge of the return special to Blackburn titled 'The Fenman'. It is passing Pye Junction on the Nottingham - Chesterfield section. As 1984 drew to a close, the Gresley Pacific was about to be dismantled for its mandatory 7-year overhaul. Dare we all hope that it might emerge for its next stint of BR service in BR livery as No 60103 and sporting German smoke deflectors? *(Peter J C Skelton)*

Clan Line returns

Right: A £30 000 overhaul of the magnificent *Clan Line* was completed in 1984, allowing it to return to BR metals. 27 July saw it tested on a trial 9-coach train from Swindon to Bath and return. It achieved the national television news the same evening for it set fire to the lineside in numerous locations. Indeed, the trial run brought no credit to the locomotive, for it was pictured on television clearly being hurried along, despite the obvious need for caution in view of the drought. The heat of the day is evident in this picture of exhaust-less No 35028 passing Acton Turville on its test run. *(Peter J C Skelton)*

Above: The thoroughness of the restoration of *Clan Line* can be gleaned from this photograph of the 'Merchant Navy' on its first revenue-earning run, which took place on 29 September when it hauled the 'Welsh Marches Express' from Hereford to Chester and return. It is seen approaching Ruabon on the return journey. The firm of Resco undertook much of the repair work to *Clan Line's* tender during the locomotive's three-year overhaul. *(Peter J C Skelton)*

Left: No 35028 did not venture away from the North & West route during 1984, working only the WMEs. In this view *Clan Line* was on duty south of Hereford and is pictured in a sylvan setting at Abergavenny on 20 October. *(Jim Coleman)*

West Highland steam revival

Right: Steam returned to the West Highland Extension after 21 years on 24 May when 'Black Five' No 5407 worked a 4-coach press special to Mallaig to signal the start of a highly successful season which, once again, was underestimated by BR. The North British Railway 0-6-0 No 673 *Maude* made its debut on the branch on 28 May when it hauled a 4-coach 'West Highlander' SLOA-organised special. Difficulties en route with the veteran resulted in the train being terminated at Arisaig. Epitomising the return of steam to this highly scenic line is this view of Glenfinnan viaduct with No 673 *Maude* on its return journey on 28 May. *(Mrs Mary Boocock)*

Right. *Maude* proved to be not quite up to the demands of the Fort William-Mallaig gradients during its stint on the new steam service. Its first day ended in disgrace when it caused fires and suffered poor timekeeping. But did anyone really mind? This delightful 0-6-0 is seen at the end of 28 May at Fort William. *(Colin Boocock)*

Below: This view taken on 27 May shows No 5407 running round its train at Mallaig, the first train to arrive at the terminus in 21 years. More than 12 000 people participated in the steam services on this line during the year under review, boosting figures by 20 per cent. By the end of the year, ScotRail had already decided that instead of the three days per week service run in 1984, 1985 would see a five-day service run from Sundays to Thursdays from 17 June to 8 September. *(Les Nixon)*

Above: Two 'Black Fives' shared the honours of providing the staple power for the Fort William-Mallaig steam services for which the fare was a £3 return or £2 single supplement on the normal fare. No 5407 worked the first part of the season with No 44767 *George Stephenson* providing power for the latter. Sporting a blue numberplate and a 65J shed plate, No 44767 approaches Mallaig on 1 August. *(Chris Burton)*

Left: The diesels' livery and blank headcode panels give the game away that this picture is not from the early 1960s. Yes, this is Eastfield depot and this combination was once a familiar sight. It was recreated on Sunday 20 May when 'Black Five' No 5407 was en route to Fort William to work the summer service on the Mallaig line. The Class 27s are Nos 27049 (left) and 27030 *(Tom Noble)*

The hugely successful revival of steam running
between Fort William and Mallaig in May
1984 allowed photographers to exploit fully the
magnificent West Highland scenery. This is
'Black Five' No 5407 heading for Mallaig at
Lochailort on 27 May. *(Les Nixon)*

Above: A surprise return to the main line in 1984 was the Webb 0-6-2T No 1054 which was given permission by BR to haul a programme of one-coach trips from Manchester Victoria to Newton Heath as part of the 150th anniversary celebrations of Wilson's Brewery. The trips ran on Wednesdays from 6 June through to 22 August and the Caledonian Saloon No 41, based at Steamtown Carnforth, was used for passenger accommodation. The 1888-built tank is seen standing at Manchester Victoria on 20 June. *(Hugh Ballantyne)*

Below: Ian Storey's unique Stephenson link motion Stanier 'Black Five' emerged looking smart in later BR lined black livery early in 1984. This view of No 44767 coming round the curve at Clapham with the 'Cumbrian Mountain Express' on 31 March shows well the blue background to the smokebox numberplate and the 'Fort William' bufferbeam legend in readiness for the West Highland duties later in the year. *(Hugh Ballantyne)*

Above: The return of main line running of the popular *Clan Line* revived impressive scenes such as this one, with the Pacific passing Church Stretton with a southbound 'Welsh Marches Express' on a crisp 10 November. *(Hugh Ballantyne)*

Below: With 'Jubilee' No 5690 *Leander* based on the Severn Valley line, its 'home' BR route is now the North & West line. Its first outing in 1984 was on 18 February. Providing a view which explains why this machine is one of the all-time favourites, No 5690 is seen near Pontypool Road. *(John Chalcraft)*

Above: On its first revenue-earning run in England since preservation, A4 Pacific No 60009 *Union of South Africa* passes Barons Wood with the southbound 'Cumbrian Mountain Express' on 31 March. *(Hugh Ballantyne)*

Below: Lamentably *Union of South Africa* was only used twice on the 'Scarborough Spa Express' circular working. It is seen approaching Harrogate on the morning outward leg from York on 9 August. *(Les Nixon)*

Haste ye back

Left: No 60009 headed south in 1984 to work two Settle & Carlisle runs in each direction and two 'Scarborough Spa Expresses'. Once again the opportunity was taken to work a locomotive to Carlisle by means of passenger duty between Ayr and Carlisle. No 60009 reached Carlisle by hauling 'The Sou-Wester Express' on 10 March and the train is depicted at Ayr with the expected loyal gathering of devotees. *(D J Howdle)*

Above: For many people 31 March was the day to head for the Settle & Carlisle for inspiration and rejuvenation. No 9 was coming and it was not to be missed. It was nearly two decades since the most popular of all the preserved A4s last set foot on English metals. This picture shows *Union of South Africa* returning in triumph in Waitby cutting. *(Mick Roberts)*

Left: Surely the best locomotive yet to visit Scarborough on the 'Scarborough Span Express'? John Cameron's magnificent No 60009 *Union of South Africa* worked two Scarborough trips during its lamentably short stay south of the Border. Indeed, its owner and dedicated attendants were known to be disappointed with the amount of working allocated to No 9 considering the vast amount of work and organisation that had to be expended to permit this famous A4 to work south. Proving that Sir Nigel Gresley knew how to write poetry, or at least make it move, is this study of No 9 proudly bearing its Scottish ancestry at Scarborough on 14 August. *(R L Patrick)*

Leeds-Hull anniversary

1984 was the 150th anniversary of the Leeds-Selby line and to commemorate this event the West Yorkshire County Council ran 'The West Yorkshire Enterprise' on 22 September using recently overhauled Class A4 No 4498 *Sir Nigel Gresley* on an itinerary from Leeds to Scarborough via Hull. This took No 4498 off its usual routes and these pictures show the train arriving in Selby en route to Hull and climbing northwards from Bempton on the single line section from Bridlington to Seamer. *(Peter Marsh; Hugh Ballantyne)*

A RAILWAY DIARY FOR 1984

Compiled by Howard Johnston

JANUARY

2. Ayr depot fire, £1.6 million damage to buildings and dmu stock.

5. Goole-Gilberdyke route closure plans announced.

5. Telephone service inaugurated on Paddington-Swansea HST service. Cost of a call, 50p.

5. Ayrshire lines £3 million resignalling contract (linked to electrification) signed.

5. Strathclyde PTE investment and cost-cutting plan announced. Widespread line and service cuts to reflect falling demand.

16. Bishops Stortford-Cambridge electrification authorised. Completion expected in 1988.

16. Modernised Cardiff Central concourse opened by Viscount Tonypandy.

17. Massive dmu replacement policy announced, but work to be put out for tender instead of going automatically to BREL.

17. Scottish locomotive 26044 destroyed by fire in a snowdrift... dampness caused a traction motor flashover between Dalwhinnie and Blair Atholl, and fire brigade unable to get near.

18. 100th birthday of George Spiller, thought to be last survivor to have worked with steam on LT District Line.

18. Door missing from HST on Bristol-Weston-super-Mare service. Found in St Philips Marsh washing plant.

21. Worst day of Scottish blizzards, leading to helicopter rescue for stranded West Highland Line passengers.

21. National Settle and Carlisle rescue campaign opens with petition to 10 Downing Street.

21. HST power car 43049 named *Neville Hill*, first of a series to commemorate East Coast maintenance depots.

22. New alignment of North Wales Coast line at Colwyn Bay brought into full use.

23. Full Bedford-St Pancras/Moorgate electric service finally gets underway.

27. Public meeting organised to rescue threatened Goole-Gilberdyke route.

27. Conversion of closed Manchester-Sheffield route via Woodhead to a road rejected by Transport Minister on cost grounds.

28. Executive saloon 40513 exhibited. Hire is £200 single journey, plus first class fare.

28. 60th birthday of Isle of Wight's ex-London Transport tube car S43,

Llandudno Jct-Crewe dmu, using the new North Wales Coast route alignment at the site of former Mochdre and Pabo station on 5 February. The old trackbed was to form the course of A55 road improvement. *(D C Gatehouse)*

InterCity Executive Saloon No 40513 on display at Nottingham Midland in May. *(Gary Grafton)*

marked by special run between Ryde and Shanklin.

31. Paddington crash loco 50041 *Bulwark* arrives at Doncaster Works for repair.

31. Railfreight decides on £55 000 National Hunt racing sponsorship.

31. First parts of dismantled Beyer Peacock-Garratt steam locomotive arrive at Greater Manchester Museum from South Africa.

FEBRUARY

3. Freightliner driver and guard killed in collision between two trains on same line at Wigan.

4. Waterloo Area Resignalling Scheme commissioned.

6. BRE-Leyland "economy" Class 141 demonstration railbus leaves for Thailand.

6. Radipole station, former halt for Weymouth's steam depot, closed permanently because of unsafe platforms.

11. Darlington North Road museum first phase opened.

13. WR moves into new Swindon HQ, to be named 125 House. Paddington, Reading, Cardiff and Bristol Divisions run down.

14. Withdrawal at Crewe of Great Train Robbery locomotive 40126. Destined for Doncaster Works for rapid dismantling.

20. First passenger service for a decade on Churnet Valley Line to Oakamoor organised by North Staffs Railway.

21. Last workable AC diesel railbus changes hands again, this time to Colne Valley Railway. Had been sold by North Yorkshire Moors Railway to Kent and East Sussex in 1980.

25. Locomotive 50007 re-christened *Sir Edward Elgar* at Paddington to mark 50th anniversary of composer's death. Worked 1215 Paddington-Oxford, and fails on return trip.

MARCH

1. Chesterfield's by-election fails to win a House of Commons seat for Helen Anscomb and her Death off Roads, Freight on

171

Rail Party. Polls 34 votes to winner Tony Benn's 24 633.

3. CIE (Eire) takes delivery of first of 124 Mark 3-based coaches from BREL Derby Litchurch Lane Works.

5. Sheffield-Penistone subsidy renewed by South Yorkshire County Council on short term basis.

7. Start on new spur at Lincoln, crossing the path of the closed avoiding line to eliminate St Marks station and concentrate traffic on Central.

10. London depots honoured by twin naming ceremony of HST power car 43057 *Bounds Green* and 47408 *Finsbury Park*.

15. Marylebone closure plans announced, but date dependent on outcome of public inquiry.

17. Consett branch closure marked by special Derwentside Rail Action Group passenger train hauled by 46026 *Leicestershire and Derbyshire Yeomanry*.

18. LT Bakerloo train runs for eight miles from Queens Park depot and through six stations without its driver. Inquiry launched.

19. First Class 141 railbus handed over to South Yorkshire PTE by BR Chairman Bob Reid. Twenty sets intended for Leeds-York and Leeds-Harrogate services.

19. Open station concept extended to Southampton-Weymouth, Basingstoke-Exeter, Exeter-Sherbourne, Weymouth-Yeovil-Bristol, Salisbury-Bristol (except Bath), and Newbury-Taunton.

23. Tyne and Wear Metro final section between Heworth and South Shields (eight miles) officially opened.

24. £1.7 million Section 8 grants to English China Clays and Bardon Hill Quarries, Leicestershire and West Drayton.

26. Mixed freight/passenger service restarts between Aberdeen and Wick.

26. Vote of no confidence by BR in future of Reedham-Yarmouth route.

28. Day of Action in support of Greater London Council halts all LT services.

28. End of diesel-hydraulic era on BR – at least until 8 June and the Class 150 unveiling! – with withdrawal of final displaced Bedford-St Pancras Class 127 dmus from Barking-Gospel Oak service.

Class 127 2-car set M51649/M51627 forms the 1045 Gospel Oak-Barking at Junction Road Junction on 12 March. *(J Critchley)*

Superficially not an obvious choice for electrification, this is Southminster, hosting 31222 on nuclear flask duty on 6 September. BR in April announced plans to wire up the 16½-mile branch from Wickford by May 1986. *(I C Scotchman)*

31. A4 60009 *Union of South Africa* returns to England to work 'Cumbrian Mountain Express' over Settle and Carlisle route.

APRIL

2. Opening of new Swindon freight depot.

2. Swansea's enlarged travel centre brought into use.

7. Ipswich loses semaphore signals as part of electrification remodelling.

8. Isle of Wight takes delivery of new yard shunter 03079 (97805) from Sealink ferry, replacement for withdrawn 97803 (05001) sold for preservation on the island.

9. Saltaire station (closed 1965) reopened by West Yorkshire PTE.

9. Mallaig depot closure plans withdrawn. £1.8 million steamer pier extension also planned.

14. Last Sykes lock-and-block instruments taken out of use at Charing (SR) signalbox

15. 1958 Swedish 205hp diesel railbus delivered to Nene Valley Railway.

16. Hamburger revolution reaches Manchester Piccadilly with opening of new Casey Jones takeaway bar.

18. First day of Class 141 services in West Yorkshire.

18. New station opened at Auchinleck, Ayrshire.

18. Preserved 'Green Goddess' Class 40 40106 delivered to the Great Central Railway.

21. First passenger train on new Peak Railway, Hunslet 0-6-0ST in Buxton yard.

22. Transport Minister Nicholas Ridley opens Gloucestershire and Warwickshire Railway at ceremony at Toddington.

24. Four acres of forest destroyed by fire next to the Settle and Carlisle line at Armathwaite. Steam special locomotive 60009 *Union of South Africa* blamed.

25. Rail Union Federation (NUR and ASLEF) advocate £3000 million ten-year rail investment plan, to save £250 million a year thereafter.

26. First-ever Class 27 locomotives arrive at Swindon for repairs.

26. Cable thieves throw Edinburgh-Glasgow push-pull service into chaos.

29. 125th anniversary of Brunel's Saltash bridge marked by special train and unveiling of plaque.

30. Severn Railway reaches £300 000 share issue for new Kiddersminster railhead.

MAY

1. Spectacular crash at Carlisle – runaway Freightliner vehicles switched to avoiding lines and into the River Caldew.

1. New Victoria signalling centre officially opened.

2. New 1983 stock enters service on LT Jubilee line. Fifteen six-car sets ordered from Metro-Cammell/BREL.

7. Vale of Rheidol gala day with all three steam locomotives in action.

9. Oxford Cowley freight terminal reopened with £180 000 grant. Ten thousand lorry journeys saved.

10. Inaugural run of 'Gatwick Express' push-pull service from Victoria behind Executive-liveried electro-diesel 73123, thus named for the occasion.

11. Severn Valley Railway's first rail trip into Kidderminster – a train load of concrete sleepers over new track giving direct access to the station yard.

11. Executive locomotive liveries unveiled on West Coast electrics 87006 *City of Glasgow* and 87012 *Couer-de-Lion*.

12. First Class 50 visit to Scarborough – 50043 *Eagle* used on railtour.

12. Tamworth Rail Week sees first Class 25 named, 25322, reinstated with new livery to become *Tamworth Castle*.

During its pioneering run to Scarborough on 12 May, No 50043 *Eagle* passed the famous Haxby distant. *(David Stacey)*

12. Bedford St Johns station closed to be replaced by new station 250 yards to the north two days later, providing better service on Bletchley line.

12. Class 40 Preservation Society accepts ownership of 40145 at Bury Transport Museum.

13. Last day of Swindon-built Class 123 and 124 dmus on the Trans-Pennine Hull-Liverpool route.

13. Kettering-Peterborough coach link axed through poor patronage.

14. New Westbury power box commissioned.

14. Closure of Bradford Hammerton Street depot, first diesel maintenance centre in West Yorkshire, opened in 1958. Darlington likewise.

14. Video coach launched on Glasgow-Edinburgh push-pull service.

14. Reopening of Lostock Hall station (Preston) after 15 years. Preston Road station on the Liverpool-Kirby route renamed Rice Lane.

14. Timetable changes:

Eastern Region. More intensive HST working removes locomotive-hauled workings south of York except local commuter trains. Kings Cross-Edinburgh times cut to all-time record 270 min for 393-mile journey; South Trans-Pennines remodelled; East Suffolk loses through services.

Western Region. Longer turn-round for HSTs to reduce risk of failure through overwork; return to high capacity locomotive-hauled for Paddington-Penzance high summer workings; new Paddington-Hull service; HSTs to Oxford and Malvern.

London Midland Region. West Coast Main Line speed-up with first 110mph 'Royal Scot', 5 hr 5 min London-Glasgow; Midland Main Line reliefs to cope with extra business; HSTs diagrammed to Manchester and Liverpool on services from WR.

Southern Region. Gatwick Express launched; Brighton line speed-up, but massive cuts in off-peak services.

Scottish Region. New Highland Chieftain HST to Inverness; more far North and West Highland speed-ups.

14. Demise of the vacuum-braked wagonload train.

14. Passenger services restored to Copy Pit route with grant from National and Provincial Building Society.

14. Reopening of Sandwell and Dudley station on the Birmingham-Wolverhampton line.

14. Last Mark 1 sleepers retired from Scottish Region service.

14. Sleeper prices slashed for full-fare ticket holders on West of England services.

17. Settle and Carlisle closure notice reissued after previous notice disallowed. 2500 protest total reached.

18. Death at Newmarket of famous racehorse St Paddy, inspiration for name of Class 55 Deltic locomotive 55001.

21. Industrial action disrupts South Yorkshire services as signalmen sympathise with striking miners.

24. Royal Assent for new Manchester routes – link between Styal Loop between Heald Green and Styal to Manchester airport, and Hazel Grove chord from Stockport Edgeley Junction to the Heaton Mersey-New Mills section of the former Midland main line.

24. West Highland steam service from Fort William to Mallaig reinaugurated by LMS Class 5 4-6-0 5407.

25. Opening of South Tynedale Railway at Alston, 2ft gauge on route closed by BR in May 1976.

30. Sealink services halted for 48 hr in protest to sell-off to private industry. Townsend Thorensen and P & O pull out in sympathy.

30. World's first credit card ticket machine opened at Euston station, intended to reduce queuing.

31. Fifteen-year deal signed to move by rail 150 000 tons, half of Avon's annual rubbish quota, to dump in Buckinghamshire.

31. Death of Derek Cross, railway photographer and writer.

JUNE

1. £25 million investment agreed for 75 new Class 150 dmus.

1. Tenth anniversary of reopening of Kent and East Sussex Railway.

2. Crewe and Derby Works open days.

2. West Yorkshire PTE Class 141 dmu makes goodwill visit to Keighley and Worth Valley Railway.

2. SR King Arthur steam locomotive 777 *Sir Lamiel* pressed into BR service on York-Harrogate-Leeds route after dmu fails on departure.

4. Prince Michael of Kent opens Amberley Chalk Pits Museum half-mile passenger railway.

6. 'Northern Belle' summer excursions start on the Dufftown branch.

6. ScotRail sees first refurbished Class 303 emu in orange and black livery at Glasgow Central.

6. LNWR 'Coal Tank' 1054 works brewery-sponsored specials from Manchester Victoria to Miles Platting.

8. First Class 150 'Sprinter' dmu unveiled at York Works.

11. New Westbury travel centre opened.

14. New design electric railcar delivered to Blackpool Tramway.

16. BR gets approval to spend £14.7 million on 15 more Class 58 locomotives, bringing the fleet total to 50.

16. Locomotive 37017 becomes BR's most northern-travelled locomotive when it overruns the buffer stops at Thurso.

18. Demolition of disused 1864 Thames bridge at Blackfriars starts.

20. West Midlands PTE opens discussions on rapid transit system, with new routes, part-electrification, and part-bus-replacement.

23. Newlyweds Diane and Tony Parkins hire locomotive 31117 and 1926 WR inspection saloon for honeymoon trip from High Wycombe to Shrewsbury.

24. Morpeth derailment. Brand new Mark 3 sleepers in 1950 Aberdeen-Kings Cross destroyed. No fatalities, but 38 injured.

24. Experimental Maidenhead-Marlow Sunday service restarts after 25 years.

25. Eastern Region management changes see five regional and 32 area offices reduced to 18 area offices responsible directly to York.

26. Former Ashford Works site put up for sale.

27. Trials on West Wales routes with 350 hp Class 08 shunter 08259 with cut-down cab designed as 204 hp Class 03 replacement.

29. Plans shown for £20 million complex at Oxford station site as part of redevelopment plans.

JULY

1. Corby sees first passenger train for 18 years, excursion to Scarborough.

No 08259 with cut-down cab to work limited clearance Gwendraeth Valley line on a test run to Cwmmawr on 16 July. Two more 08s were to be similarly treated, signalling the end of the 03s in South Wales. *(BR Cardiff)*

BREL's export design 'International' coach, unveiled on 4 July. *(BR)*

4. 'International' coach shown by BREL to foreign buyers at Derby Litchurch Lane Works. Plans for ten-coach International rake built to BR gauge to run on West Coast Main Line. Gabon (West Africa) places £3.5 million order for ten coaches and timber wagons.

4. 2000th Lackenby-Workington steel train celebrated by naming of locomotive 37078 *Teesside Steelmaster*.

4. New three-track depot opened at Chappel and Wakes Colne, headquarters of Stour Valley Railway.

6. 1045 Inverness-Kyle of Lochalsh hauled by newly-named 37260 *Radio Highland* inaugurates the route's radio electronic token block signalling system. Twenty signal jobs cut to three. Occasion also used to demonstrate videos on trains prior to October introduction on 'Starlight Express' service.

8. More WR stations go 'open', Cheltenham, Gloucester-Caldicot, Swindon-Kemble, Bedminster-Weston-super-Mare.

9. London Transport bans smoking on trains.

9. Trial reopening of Sherburn-in-Elmet station, between York and Sheffield.

14. GWR 1902 100 mph record breaker 4-4-0 3717 *City of Truro* moved from Swindon to Severn Valley Railway for renovation for GWR 150 celebrations.

15. Return to service on West Somerset Railway of pioneer preserved Swindon Class 14 D9526.

17. CEGB stage 100 mph collision with nuclear flask at Old Dalby test track. Locomotive 46009 destroyed, flask stays intact.

18. Class 141 dmu demonstrated on Liskeard-Looe line as prelude to 13 production units arriving in Cornwall in 1985.

18. First Class 15 D8233 (lately heating unit ADB968001) secured for preservation at Chapeltown, Sheffield.

19. Tonbridge-Hastings electrification scheme inaugurated with 'gold' insulator installed at Robertsbridge. Completion target of the £24 million 31-mile project, May 1986.

21. Remote Sugar Loaf halt on Swansea-Shrewsbury route (closed 1965) reopened as summer tourist halt.

BRB Chairman Bob Reid samples train-borne video on 6 July during events to mark launch of Kyle-Dingwall radio signalling. *(Peter Fox)*

22. Resignalling at Spalding eliminates all semaphore signalling in the area.

23. First track panel laid for £185 000 Nene Valley Railway extension into Peterborough City centre.

23. Electric APT runs trial on East Coast Main Line from Newcastle – propelled of course.

23. New station opened at South Bank, Teesside.

24. Scarborough Council agrees to pay for £35 000 restoration of world steam speed record holder, A4 Pacific 4468 *Mallard*.

24. LMS Black Five 4-6-0 5305 named *Alderman A. E. Draper* at York to commemorate the late Hull scrapyard owner who reprieved it from the torch in 1969.

27. East Coast Main Line electrification approved. Hitchin-Leeds and Edinburgh in £306 million plan, projected completion date May 1991.

27. Restored Bullied Merchant Navy 4-6-2 35028 *Clan Line* makes inaugural run after overhaul in steam from Swindon to Bristol and sets fire to acres of lineside.

28. Manningtree signal box closed, control transferred to Colchester power box.

28. Doncaster Works open day.

30. Polmont crash. Thirteen die when 1730 Glasgow-Edinburgh push-pull express collides with stray cow. Worst death toll since Hither Green, 1967.

30. Steam returns to Kidderminster with opening of Severn Valley extension from Bewdley. Locomotive used, 4930 *Hagley Hall*.

30. Watercress Line carries its 500 000th passenger since reopening on 30 April 1977.

31. First steaming of ex-Barry Standard Class 4 2-6-0 75069 at Bridgnorth, Severn Valley Railway.

HLPG 'Black Five' No 5305, named *Alderman A. E. Draper* on 24 July, leaves York on the 'Scarborough Spa Express' on 26 August. *(E A J Saunders)*

AUGUST

1. Birtley, Newcastle, derailment. Four coaches of 0730 Leeds-Edinburgh HST slip down embankment. No serious casualties, poor track maintenance blamed.

1. Plym Valley Railway's newly-arrived South African Railways Beyer-Garratt 4-8-2+2-8-4 4112 named *Springbok*.

4. UK's last regularly working industrial steam locomotive retired. Andrew Barclay 0-4-0ST 1823 *Harry* moved from Crossley's scrapyard at Shipley, West Yorks to Peak Railway, Buxton.

4. Preserved Great Central Railway Class 40 40106 named *Atlantic Conveyer* to commemorate Falklands campaign.

5. First August Sunday special calls at Dunrobin station on the Far North line, former private halt of the Duke of Sutherland.

5. Gatwick push-pull services temporarily withdrawn after Class 73 locomotive fires. Stock withdrawn for examination.

6. Workmen acting for the High Court move into closed Ashford Steam Centre to scrap fireless locomotive and Bulleid double-decker emu coach.

13. Demolition starts of LSWR Weymouth station buildings.

15. Official opening of refurbished Swansea station.

20. LT driver killed in Central Line collision in open section at Leyton, scene of a similar accident in January 1979.

21. Joint-funded Shildon Forge Ltd opened in former BREL premises.

22. Contracts awarded for £60 million Docklands Light Railway. Completion target July 1987.

28. Pair of Riddles-design WD 2-10-0s return from Greece to Ipswich with American S160 2-8-0. Destined for Mid-Hants and Lavender Lines.

30. World diesel journey speed record (117.6 miles Paddington-Bristol in 62 min 33 sec, average 112.8 mph) set by HST set 253001. Power car 43002 named *Top of the Pops* to mark its role in live TV show.

SEPTEMBER

1. Plans laid for new Fairbourne Railway station with the name Gorsafawddacha'-idraigddanheddogleddolonpenrhynare-urdraethceredigion. Honest.

1. Settle-Carlisle Joint Action Committee becomes limited company with £55 000 annual budget.

1. First run in preservation for Class 42 'Warship' diesel-hydraulic D832 *Onslaught* at Bury Transport Museum.

1. First Class 58 visit to West Country when 58002 borrowed to tow failed HST

into Plymouth on 1V87 1210 Liverpool-Penzance service.

3. Melton station on East Suffolk line reopened after 29 years.

4. Preservationists outbid for last BR Class 24, electric-heating unit 24142 (ADB968009). Broken up instead at Cooper's scrapyard, Attercliffe, Sheffield.

7. Loaned Kent and East Sussex 112-year-old LB&SCR 'Terrier' 0-6-0T 32670 is star attraction in steam at GWS Didcot Railway Centre.

14. Class 86 electric locomotive 86316 named *Wigan Pier* to mark rail's strong links with the town. (Locomotive later transferred to Great Eastern).

15. Dyce (Aberdeen) station reopened. Had been closed on 6 May 1968.

17. Class 40 prototype D200 damaged in shunting collision at Guide Bridge.

21. Plans for new Gloucester Barnwood station revealed, for possible start in 1987.

21. Renovated gravestone of ASLEF union founder Charles Perry rededicated in special service.

23. Ex-Southern Railway 2-BIL electric unit 2090's first public run for 13 years on excursion from Brighton to Waterloo and Portsmouth. Paired with BR's operational green 4-SUB 4732.

23. Neville Hill depot open day gives HST power car 43077 longest, and most politically controversial nameplate yet, *West Yorkshire Metropolitan County*.

26. Prime Minister Margaret Thatcher visits the National Railway Museum.

26. New Paddington parcels depot opened.

27. 160 people all with the surname Honeycombe alight from special at Plymouth to take part in family reunion.

29. Ex-Barry GWR 0-6-0PT 9681 back in service at Dean Forest Railway.

30. Sleights-Whitby singled.

Pre-heat unit ADB968009 (ex-24142) at Tinsley behind 47311 on 29 August en route to Cooper's Metals Ltd for breaking. *(Gavin Morrison)*

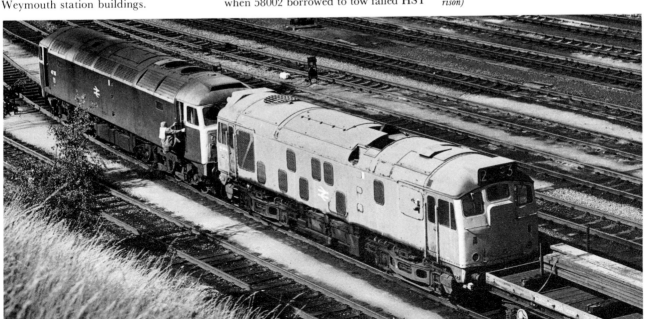

1. SR back-tracks on May timetable cuts by alterations to reduce overcrowding.

1. Brighton signalbox fire throws Central Division's services into chaos for three weeks.

1. Open station concept extended to Leicester, Derby, Nottingham areas.

1. Euston 2300 and Glasgow Central 2215 departures christened 'Starlight Express', together with locomotive 86231, after the London stage show. Services also show video films.

1. Re-opened Copy Pit route gets six Leeds-Preston through services. Yorkshire and Lancashire mayors exchange roses.

1. Cardiff Valleys timetables remodelled with extra peak services, but loss of almost all Sunday morning workings.

1. New 6S57 1945 Willesden-Mossend is 150th Speedlink service.

1. New station opened at Dunston, Newcastle.

1. Dorridge derailment. Thirty hurt when 47331-hauled Manchester-Gatwick leaves the rails at speed. Coaches stay upright because empty car wagons were parked in siding alongside.

1. HST programmed to work to Milford Haven on extended 1720 ex-Paddington.

1. Non-smoking accommodation extended on High Speed Trains.

3. Inquiry into proposed closure of London Broad Street station.

4. Fenchurch Street redevelopment scheme with offices gets underway. Project includes extended concourse, but historic facade retained.

6. New unstaffed station opened at Muireston, Livingston, Scottish Region.

7. Famous North Eastern slotted post signal at Haxby felled for display at York station forecourt.

11. Wembley Central crash. Three killed as crowded 1754 Euston-Bletchley commuter train collides with rear of Freightliner. Units 310067/86 damaged and many main line services diverted to Paddington, St Pancras and Kings Cross.

11. New locomotive depot opened at Thornton, Fife, to replace Dunfermline Townhill. Predecessor was closed 11 years before.

14. Kings Lynn-Magdalen Road singled.

17. Altnabreac, south of Wick, in the middle of moorland and without road access is labelled BR's least used station with only one passenger most weeks. On this date, seven passengers include ScR General Manager Chris Green.

18. BR Corporate Plan talks of big cuts in subsidies and loss of 13 000 jobs by 1990. Plans admit 1984 targets wrecked by miners' dispute.

18. ASLEF union gives £2500 backing to Settle and Carlisle campaign.

18. Amended Huddersfield-Penistone closure notice issued.

21. New Ashford signal control panel brought into use.

21. 75th anniversary celebration of Stephenson Locomotive Society.

22. One-man operation extended to LT Circle Line.

25. Wine merchants Harveys buy last unpreserved GWR King 4-6-0 6023 *King Edward II* for £21 000 for restoration in spare bay at Bristol Temple Meads station.

28. Four Class 86 electric locomotives begin crew-training on Great Eastern lines.

31. ScotRail's new locomotive livery seen for the first time on 47708 *Waverley* outshopped from Crewe Works.

NOVEMBER

7. Locomotive 58020 named *Doncaster Works BREL*.

8. York's new £950 000 travel centre opened. Transport Minister Nicholas Ridley names shunter 08525 *Percy the Pilot*. Unhappy crews remove the plates after he leaves.

8. 141st anniversary of extension of S&D line to Newton Aycliffe marked by naming ceremony of 47407 *Aycliffe*.

10. Freshly overhauled GWR Pannier Tank 6412 celebrates 50th anniversary with special train on West Somerset Railway, which also talks of first ever operating surplus for 1984.

12. 100 mph running introduced on Highland Main Line between Kingussie and Kincraig.

12. Ayrshire and Glasgow Clydeside outer suburban stations declared 'open'.

12. New station opened at Humphrey Park, Manchester.

12. LT shows off 1938-stock unit restored to original red livery. Although in normal service, preservation is in prospect.

18. Heath Junction, Cardiff remodelled. Heath Low and High Level stations get extra car parks.

19. BR talks of £360 million investment to replace entire dmu fleet by 1990.

20. Gresley A3 Pacific 4472 *Flying Scotsman* conveys the Queen Mother to North Woolwich to open railway museum.

21. Hove resignalling operative as latest stage of Brighton area revamp.

23. LT services disrupted by fire at Oxford Circus.

24. Steam open days to test reaction to setting up Chatham Docks steam railway.

25. BR hires Pullmans for Sunday excursion to Norwich.

25. Last Class 46 locomotives withdrawn from service. 46035/45 retained for Derby RTC experiments, flagship 46026

Specially prepared Class 116 dmus C330 and C333 at Mountain Ash station with BR-organised shoppers' and sports fans' special over the freight-only Aberdare line on 1 December. *(Deryck W Lewis)*

Leicestershire and Derbyshire Yeomanry sent to Doncaster Works for breaking up.

29. Princess Anne visits renovated Liverpool Lime Street station.

29. 0705 Hereford-Paddington derailed near Pershore on single line section. 47500 *Great Western* hauling train. No serious casualties.

DECEMBER

1. Aberdare station reopened for Saturday experiment and repeated on 15 December.

2. Collapse of retaining wall near Hampstead Heath station disrupts North London locals and inter-regional freight services for some days.

4. Salford crash. Driver and guard killed as 1005 Liverpool-Scarborough collides with rear of tank train. Passenger locomotive 45147, badly damaged, is first of eth-fitted Class 45/1 to be withdrawn.

7. BR's last 1500 V dc passenger line between Manchester and Hadfield converted to 25 kV. Last LNER stock, Class 506 units, withdrawn with passing of 1815 ex-Manchester Piccadilly.

7. End of Class 508s on SR with transfer of final examples to Merseyside.

9. De-named 87023, ex-*Highland Chieftain* runs into ole maintenance train at Rugby. No casualties but incident frustrates BR plan to rename the 87 *Royal Mail Midlands* in 1985.

11. The world's oldest international newspaper celebrates 250th anniversary with naming of 47574 *Lloyds List* at Liverpool Street station.

12. Euston-Glasgow speed record of 3 hr 52¾ min set up by APT despite signal check at Trent Valley.

31. BR announces all but three of surviving 17 Class 40s to be withdrawn from 20 January 1985.